From "A Horse of the Hash-Knife Brand" in the *San Francisco Examiner*,
February 15, 1891.

ROUGH RIDER

Buckey O'Neill of Arizona

DALE L. WALKER

UNIVERSITY OF NEBRASKA PRESS
LINCOLN AND LONDON

Flagstaff Public Library
Flagstaff, Arizona

© 1975 Dale L. Walker
Preface to the Bison Books edition ©1997 by the University of Nebraska Press
All rights reserved
Manufactured in the United States of America

⊖ The paper in this book meets the minimum requirements of American National
Standard for Information Sciences—Permanence of Paper for Printed Library
Materials, ANSI Z39.48-1984.

First Bison Books printing: 1997
Most recent printing indicated by the last digit below:
10   9   8   7   6   5   4   3   2   1

Library of Congress Cataloging-in-Publication Data
Walker, Dale L.
[Death was the black horse]
Rough Rider: Buckey O'Neill of Arizona / Dale L. Walker.
p.   cm.
Originally published: Death was the black horse. Austin, Tex.:
Madrona Press, 1975.
Includes bibliographcal references and index.
ISBN 0-8032-9796-3 (pbk.: alk. paper)
1. O'Neill, William Owen, 1860–1898.   2. United States.   Army.
Volunteer Cavalry, 1st—Biography.   3. Pioneers—Arizona—Biography.
4. Soldiers—Arizona—Biography.   5. Spanish-American War, 1898—
Campaigns.   6. Arizona—Biography.   I. Title.
F811.05W34   1998
973.8'9'092—dc21
[B]   97-30149
             CIP

Reprinted from the original 1975 edition, titled *Death Was the Black Horse*, by
Madrona Press, Austin, Texas.

Flagstaff Public Library
Flagstaff, Arizona

A
B
0580w
1997

To Richard O'Connor

CONTENTS

ILLUSTRATIONS

PREFACE TO THE BISON BOOKS EDITION

In researching this book, as stated in the acknowledgments, I had the good fortune to interview the last three survivng members of the First U.S. Volunteer Cavalry Regiment, best known by that felicitous nickname "the Rough Riders." Sadly, two of these splendid gentlemen, Frank Brito and George Hamner, died before the book appeared, leaving Jesse D. Langdon as the Last Rough Rider and, coincidentally, the last man to have witnessed the death in Cuba, on July 1, 1898, of the book's subject, William Owen "Buckey" O'Neill.

Upon receiving my complimentary copies of the book, I dispatched one to my lifelong friend Alvin Spencer Fick, then living in Amsterdam, New York, who took it downstate to Red Hook, in South Brooklyn, to present to Mr. Langdon. Not many months before, Mr. Langdon had written me that he was anxious to read my account of the San Juan battle in which Buckey died. The ninety-four-year-old ex-trooper was delighted to have the hand-delivered book and sat in his parlor while Al Fick snapped pictures, poring over the "Up to Kettle Hill" chapter with a huge magnifying glass and pronouncing it "good and accurate."

The last letter I received from Mr. Langdon congratulated me on the book, which he said he had read "cover to cover" and which he said "educated me on that wonderful character Buckey O'Neil."

During my thirty-six years as a professional writer, nothing has pleased me more than Mr. Langdon's approval of this book.

He died on June 28, 1975, at the Veteran's Hospital in Castle Point, New York, four months after I last heard from him.

Theodore Roosevelt had a particularly warm place in his heart for Buckey O'Neill, recognizing him as a true pioneer of territorial Arizona, a great-hearted, adventuresome character, and a born soldier. There are poignant passages about O'Neill in Roosevelt's *The Rough Riders* (1900), and one senses that Buckey's death touched the future president more than any incident in his "crowded hour" in Cuba that summer of '98.

Buckey *is* an affecting character. I thought so from first to last in writing this book and wish I had known this handsome, rollicking, restless, likeable man, so greatly talented and so enormously ambitious, as T.R. did.

Published as *Death Was the Black Horse* by Madrona Press in Austin, Texas, and originally appearing in February 1975, *Rough Rider* has been out-of-print for eleven years. I am delighted to see it anew and am most grateful to the University of Nebraska Press for giving Buckey O'Neill's story this new life.

Dale L. Walker
El Paso, Texas
November 1996

PREFACE

For SIXTY-SEVEN YEARS, Solon Hannibal Borglum's powerful statue of Buckey O'Neill has drawn wondering visitors up the tree-lined walk in front of the Yavapai County Courthouse in Prescott, Arizona. The statue, with its great native granite base, stands eighteen feet high on the north side of the courthouse, corner of South Montezuma and West Gurley streets, a frozen-in-motion, Remingtonesque bronze figure astride a reined-in, straining cavalry mount whose mouth is agape at the tug against the bit, nostrils flaring from a hard ride. The rider's face is tucked leftward as if against the wind but is greatly detailed, down to the stylish military moustache; and every fold of uniform and saddle blanket, every saber nick and boot scuff, is unerringly true to life.

On September 11, 1928, twenty-one years after it was unveiled, John Gutzon de la Mothe Borglum visited Prescott and for the first time saw the work of his then-dead younger brother. He paced methodically up and down on all sides of the statue while town officials stood by. With unmistakable emotion, the Mount Rushmore sculptor said, "Although the work is the product of my brother's hand, I am forced to forget relationship and to say that the Buckey O'Neill monument is a marvel."

With the passage of years the statue is no less a marvel, but the man in whose memory it was erected has had fleeter renown: Those today whose eyes are caught by the man astride the straining horse have a common reaction and most say to themselves, "Who the hell is *that?*"

Officially, the statue is of no specific person; it is rather symbolic of the Arizonans in the Rough Riders of 1898. If you read the darkening plaques attached to its granite pedestal, you will find the words "To the Memory of" and "In Honor of," but if you will ask any Prescott citizen "Who the hell is *that?*" he will gladly tell you—"*That* is Buckey O'Neill." And he'll expect you to know who Buckey O'Neill was.

But it is only when you look at the statue *after* looking into his life that you come to appreciate who Buckey O'Neill was— and then you begin to realize that there is no end of plausible speculation on what he might have done, had he lived longer.

DALE L. WALKER
El Paso, Texas

Acknowledgments

IN 1970, WHEN I began seriously to look into Buckey O'Neill's story, I discovered there were three surviving members of the First U.S. Volunteer Cavalry Regiment (Rough Riders): Frank C. Brito of Las Cruces, New Mexico; Jesse D. Langdon of Red Hook, New York; and Dr. George Hamner of Bay Pines, Florida. In late 1970 I interviewed ninety-three-year-old Frank Brito twice and, although he knew Captain O'Neill only briefly while under his command during the Tampa turmoil preceding the embarkation to Cuba, his recollections on the regiment were quite helpful. Later, through the kindness of Jean Hamner, I was able to study the papers of Dr. Hamner, which also were illuminating.

Jesse Langdon was ninety when I contacted him through correspondence in 1971. During the months that followed I received some long and utterly priceless letters in which Langdon, a member of Woodbury Kane's K Troop, gave his eyewitness story of Buckey O'Neill's death below Kettle Hill, and a brilliant firsthand recollection of how San Juan Hill finally fell that same day.

Dr. Hamner died February 6, 1973, at the age of ninety-nine in the veterans' hospital in Bay Pines. Frank Brito died the following April 22. Jesse Langdon is the last Rough Rider.

The author is indebted to a number of persons and organizations in Arizona for their many kindnesses and aid: Maurice O'Neill of Phoenix, grandson of Buckey O'Neill; Charles Herner of Tucson, author of *The Arizona Rough Riders*; Mrs. Dora Heap, curator of the Sharlot Hall Museum in Prescott; Miss Jo Osterman, Office of the Mayor, Prescott; Bert Fireman, Arizona State University, Tempe; Mrs. Elizabeth Krakauer, Prescott

College, Prescott; the *Prescott Courier*; the Arizona Historical Society in Tucson and its chief of publications, Dr. C. L. Sonnichsen; the Phoenix Public Library; and Jim Cook of the *Arizona Republic Sunday Magazine* in Phoenix.

In El Paso I wish to thank Dr. Carl Hertzog and José Cisneros for their contributions to this book in particular and for long friendships in general; Dr. Milton Leech, Leon Metz, Dr. E. H. Antone, Dr. Haldeen Braddy, Dr. Ray Past, all of the University of Texas at El Paso, for sustained interest in the project; Russell D. Walker and James B. Murray for rare books, fine points of firearms, and military information.

Naturally I must thank my family for their patience during the work on this book: my wife, Alice McCord Walker; and my children, Dianne, Eric, Christopher, Michael, and John—all of whom got to know something about Buckey O'Neill and grew to revere him as much as I.

In far-away Decatur, Illinois, warm gratitude is extended to Mrs. Joy Ann Elliott and Mrs. Eilleen Hall for encouragement over a period of nearly forty years. Still farther away, in Amsterdam, New York, I wish to express special thanks to Alvin S. Fick, my friend of many years, whom I counted on to interview Jesse Langdon for me and who came through in impeccable style.

CHAPTER ONE

Getting to Know the Territory

 FOR ONE WHO was to become, in William Mc-
Leod Raine's words, "the most many-sided man
Arizona has produced," young William Owen
O'Neill could scarcely have made a more inauspicious entrance
into territorial history. In September, 1879, he rode a burro
through the dust down Washington Street in Phoenix looking
for work. Yet it was not quite as ludicrous or dismal a scene
as it appeared; O'Neill had ambition and prospects and he was
young—just three years older than the Territory itself.

President Lincoln had signed the statute creating Arizona
Territory on February 24, 1863, and set in motion the machinery for its government by appointing John Noble Goodwin
of Maine as the first territorial governor. The population of the
area was a slim 4,500 or so (including soldiers), but Goodwin
and the three governors who followed him, despite their short
tenures, had worked hard with their legislatures in making
something out of the trackless chunk of land under their political dominion.

By 1866, the Atlantic and Pacific Railroad, harbinger of
progress and "civilization," had received a forty-mile-wide
grant across the Territory along the famous thirty-fifth parallel.
Population was rising slowly but steadily (it was more than
forty thousand at the time O'Neill moved west). Property values
were moving upward. Cattle, wool, timber, gold, and silver were
becoming mainstay resources, and there was even speculation
that cotton, as well as a variety of edibles, might thrive in the
Salt River Valley, despite the scarcity of water.

Next to the Indians, water, or the lack of it in certain areas,

was the Territory's biggest problem. In the fall of 1880, just a
year after Buckey arrived in Phoenix, President Rutherford B.
Hayes stopped over in the little town of Maricopa, south of
Phoenix, to talk to some Apache chiefs. The President's traveling companion, General William Tecumseh Sherman, over-
heard a remark that all Arizona needed was less heat and more
water. "Huh!" snorted the general. "That's all *Hell* needs!"

In 1879, the Territory's countless miles of primitive desert
and uncharted mountain country had been carved into eight
enormous counties: Mohave and Yuma on the western side;
Yavapai, largest of them all, to the north, containing the territorial capital at Prescott; Apache, Pinal, Casa Grande, and Pima
(with Tucson as county seat); and Maricopa, shaped roughly
like a six-shooter pointed eastward with Phoenix, its county seat,
at the trigger. The Territory's governance, at the time of young
O'Neill's burro-track debut, was in doldrums. A legendary
figure of the West, now even more vainglorious and blundering
in advancing old age, was in control, but his headquarters in
Prescott was more often vacant than not. As a modern historian
of the Territory puts it, John Charles Frémont, the fifth chief
executive of Arizona, "perhaps did less for the territory than
any other governor, probably because he considered himself too
important for the position." The assessment is sadly true, and
Frémont's pathetically declining career is revealing of territorial politics at the time of O'Neill's advent.

The "Pathfinder of the West" had taken over the governorship on June 12, 1878, replacing the able John Philo Hoyt, an
Ohioan and Union Army veteran. Frémont's qualifications for
the appointment centered around his being broke because of bad
railroad investments, his need for the job, and a political debt
that President Hayes felt needed to be paid. Frémont had only
a whisper of true political credentials: in 1850 he had served
one month as senator from California but failed to retain the
seat. His political career had taken a heady upward turn, however, in 1856, when he was nominated for the presidency by the
Republican Party. Although defeated by James Buchanan, Fré-

mont compiled a creditable record—the electoral votes of eleven states and a popular vote of 1,341,000.

President Hayes, who had served under Frémont in the Valley Campaign in West Virginia during the Civil War, was a longtime admirer of the troubled explorer and felt that Frémont had saved the Republican Party in 1864 by refusing to run as a third-party candidate against Lincoln and George B. McClellan. A convention of radical Republicans, war Democrats, and various disgruntled factions had nominated Frémont in Cleveland, Ohio, that year, but Lincoln's friends delegated certain influentials (among them the poet John Greenleaf Whittier) to talk to Frémont and convince him not to divide the party. Frémont stood aside and by 1877 Hayes had been persuaded that this act was both noble and pivotal for the party, and deserving of repayment. The chance to repay came in the form of a political appointment—commonest currency on the political gaming tables then as now—which Frémont personally requested: the governorship of Arizona Territory. The salary was a meager $2,600 a year but the Pathfinder needed every penny of it.

From the start, the sixty-six-year-old Pathfinder found it difficult to stay on the path that led to the capital at Prescott. In the first place, no sooner had he moved his family to the town than his wife Jessie (Senator Thomas Hart Benton's daughter, whom Frémont had married when she was fifteen) became ill from the cold weather and high altitude. She returned to the family's Staten Island home with their son Francis, who suffered from tuberculosis. Furthermore, as Frémont addressed the Tenth Legislature in January, 1879, his hasty homework and resulting naïve proposals were met with polite disdain and ignored—except in the newspapers, where they attracted great, if somewhat sniggering, attention. He advocated establishment of a government assay office and refinery at Prescott and he was reminded that the capital was not yet a railhead. He suggested the possibility of diverting Gulf of California water into the Arizona deserts. The latter plan, although it sounded bold and flamboyant, actually was an old idea that had been dusted off periodically ever since John Wesley Powell had explored the Colorado River from its headwaters to the gulf in 1869. The best that could be said of Frémont's resurrection of the notion was that it was at least addressed to a pressing territorial problem.

The luster of having the eminent explorer-soldier in the governor's house quickly wore away, particularly in the irreverent territorial press, and the *Tucson Citizen* lost no time in observing that Frémont was "as ignorant as the Ameer of Afghanistan of Arizona affairs." Furthermore, the legislature ignored the new governor's proposals and proceeded to pass a controversial piece of legislation creating a $31,000 lottery, the professed purpose of which was to raise money for construction of government buildings and public schools.

Frémont, disclaiming any part of the lottery,[1] began a series of extended junkets eastward to visit his wife and family and to attend to personal business, concerned principally with private mining interests. He was out of the Territory six months in 1879, causing Arizona's delegate to Congress, John G. Campbell, to remark, "So far we cannot tell what sort of Governor he will make as he has spent most of his time in the East."

For the moment at least, young William O. O'Neill had little interest in this political vacuum. As soon as he climbed off the back of his burro, flipping a brown-paper cigarette into the dust, he was hired as a typesetter on the *Phoenix Herald*, a semi-weekly, four-page paper founded and managed by Charles E. McClintock. McClintock's brother Jim, also an 1879 arrival in the Territory, quickly became one of O'Neill's closest friends and confidants. Jim McClintock would share dreams of martial glory with the youngster from the East, as well as the more practical dreams of carving a career out of Arizona's sunblasted hide.

The *Herald* job, so quickly landed, unveiled the first of O'Neill's "many-sidedness" and, with a little hard cash to spend, he lost no time in unveiling yet another. Gambling in

---

[1] The lottery was repealed in 1881, after the U.S. Mails refused to pass circulars describing it. All tickets were redeemed and the Territory's pioneer merchant, Mike Goldwater (grandfather of Barry), shouldered the entire loss.

Phoenix and throughout the Territory had received legislative legality only the year before O'Neill moved West. Although gambling-hall proprietors had to pay a stiff $1,200 licensing fee, business thrived to a fare-thee-well. O'Neill, looking for some conviviality, a touch of whiskey, and above all, some action, was drawn naturally to the saloons and their games—roulette, chuck-a-luck, monte, draw poker, 7-up, and casino—and soon developed a strong liking for the saloon standby, faro. Although not yet 20, he became something of a local legend for the casual way he placed his spade bets, fearlessly "going for broke" when the hunch took hold of him. Gambling hall habitués of the day had a neat phrase for it—"bucking the tiger"— and William O. O'Neill, only a few months in the Territory, and only a few dollars in his pocket, won the appropriately gutsy nickname that soon was recognized throughout the West. When he became an officeholder, his official letters always bore the signature "W. O. O'Neill," but when he wrote to friends, it was always "Buckey."

Between chores at the *Herald* office and the turning of dealers' cards at the faro tables, Buckey periodically offered his services as special deputy to Phoenix Marshal Henry Garfias. Garfias, a tough Californian of Castilian Spanish descent, was only five years in the Territory himself. Yet he had established a reputation in Arizona, as constable and marshal, for "never going after a man that he did not return with dead or alive." There were plenty of men to go for, too. Phoenix in the 1870's had a large share of stage robbers, claim jumpers, cattle thieves, and miscellaneous gunmen, high rollers, punks, drunks, and drifters —far more than any one man, including the redoubtable Henry Garfias, could handle alone. Even hangings, half a dozen at a time, could not thin the ranks of the criminal element. A selection of headlines in Buckey's own *Herald*, gathered under the general heading, "Cavalcade of Crime," gives an indication of the work cut out for any Phoenix lawman:

A BLOODY WEEK IN PHOENIX ENDS WITH A GRAND
NECK TIE PARTY

SIX PERSONS LAUNCHED ON THEIR JOURNEY DOWN
THE DARK RIVER

JOHN LA BAR STABBED FATALLY BY A DRUNKEN RUFFIAN

JESUS FIGERO PISTOLED ON THE GILA AND ANOTHER
MEXICAN KNIFED AT SEYMOUR

MC CLOSKY AND KELLER HURRIED HELLWARD AT THE
END OF A ROPE

Garfias, a wise and sympathetic lawman, saw in O'Neill an inquiring, ambitious, adventuresome lad to whom the title of deputy marshal had an aura of romance and derring-do. The marshal delegated his chores carefully, however, and allowed little in the way of dangerous work to be anybody's responsibility but his own. Buckey, who had already come to know Phoenix's watering places, was given the job of helping round up hurrahing cowboys and miscellaneous drunks and deadbeats on Saturday night and parading them to the cooler.

Early in 1880, Buckey left his typesetting and occasional editorial job on the *Herald* when a better newspaper offer landed in his lap. He was invited to become editor of a new weekly starting up in Phoenix, the *Arizona Gazette*, founded by Charles C. and H. H. McNeil, two brothers from San Jose, California. At about the same time, when the citizenry of Phoenix organized a troop of rangers under Major C. H. Vail to pursue hostile Indians, O'Neill became one of the first men to volunteer. Volunteering for military-type activity became almost a reflex action for Buckey, although this first venture ended in his being "disappointed in seeing actual service," as Jim McClintock put it.

At least some of his military ambition could be traced to Buckey's father.

CHAPTER TWO

The O'Neills of Ireland and America

JOHN OWEN O'NEILL, Buckey's father, was born in an unidentified Irish county on August 6, 1834. There appear to be no existing records of his immigration to the United States or his occupation before 1862. One vague reference is found to his having been a farmer, another to his interest in a wholesale hardware establishment, and a third to his service in the regular army. Yet some distinct inferences can be drawn from the few known facts.

In the late 1840's, nearly 2,000,000 Irishmen died of starvation and fever as a result of the potato famine that ravaged their country. At the height of the famine, Irish immigration to America reached a peak. In one two-year period, 1847-1848, some 218,000 Irishmen fled their homes for safer shores. It is possible that among these refugees, perhaps a few years later than the mainstream, was John O. O'Neill.

As the Irish famine progressed, ship companies in search of human cargo posted placards in the country's remotest villages, advertising passage to America in the most egregious milk-and-honey terms. Passage, via Liverpool to New York or Philadelphia, cost about four pounds; the voyage took about thirty-five days, depending on the weather. Temporary buildings were erected at Ward's Island and Castle Garden, New York's main immigration ports of entry, to help the refugees. Many of them were suffering from the effects of starvation and the long voyage across the Atlantic, while many others were wracked with pain from "ship's fever," a variety of typhus.

From the beginning of the great migration, New York and Philadelphia were havens for the newly-arrived Irish. By 1870,

St. Louis ranked high in Irish-American population with 55,000 out of the 1,171,000 total citizenry. In Missouri, too, land prices were lower than in the Eastern states, with improved land available at prices ranging from $7 to $40 an acre, unimproved parcels at from $1 to $10. Farm labor also was in great demand in Missouri.

It appears that John O'Neill, on arriving in America, probably in the mid-1850's, worked on a farm near Philadelphia for another Irish immigrant family named McMenimin. Quite possibly, the farm job was waiting for him, perhaps through family connections and the institution known as the "America letter," the messages written home by immigrants urging other family members to make the American adventure. In any case, John O'Neill, on October 7, 1858, married Mary McMenimin in Philadelphia and the couple moved to St. Louis where, on February 2, 1860, their first son, William Owen, was born.

The St. Louis episode was brief, for the O'Neills again were residing in Philadelphia in the spring of 1862, when John enlisted on June 11 in Company K, 116th Pennsylvania Volunteers. The following September 1, he was mustered into service as captain, perhaps in recognition of some prior service during the period 1850-1858. A month later the 116th and the 28th Massachusetts Regiment, both largely Irish in make-up, were added to the "Irish Brigade" of Thomas Francis Meagher, known as "Meagher of the Sword."

The volatile, darkly handsome Meagher had come to America by a much more circuitous route than had John O'Neill or the others of the Irish Brigade. The son of a wealthy Irish merchant, Meagher was educated in Jesuit colleges and had been a law student at Queen's Inn in Dublin when he turned toward the revolutionary politics of the "Great Liberator," Daniel O'Connell. In 1848, Meagher was head of the Young Irish Party in Tipperary, making radical speeches against the Crown, when he was arrested for sedition, arson, and inciting a rebellion. He was sentenced to hang but Queen Victoria commuted the death sentence and ordered Meagher into exile for life on Van Dieman's Land—Tasmania—the island off the south coast of Australia. Meagher spent nearly three years in the prison colony before escaping in an open boat. By way of Brazil, he landed in May, 1852, in New York. Until the outbreak of the war, he earned a living there, writing about downtrodden Ireland and editing a newspaper called the *Irish News.*

After Fort Sumter and President Lincoln's call for seventy-five thousand volunteers, Meagher organized a Zouave company of Irishmen, the Sixty-ninth New York Infantry, which elected him a captain. One newspaperman described the Sixty-ninth as made up of "strolling vagabonds . . . picked up in the low groggeries of New York," but the raw outfit was thrown into the First Battle of Bull Run on July 21, 1861, and held together well under fire. Meagher, promoted to colonel after Bull Run, then was asked to raise a full brigade of Irish volunteers, four regiments in all. By October, 1861, the "Irish Brigade" was at full strength, and Meagher a brigadier general.

The Irishmen saw action in the Peninsular Campaign on May 31, 1862, at Fair Oaks. On July 1 they fought at Malvern Hill. By Second Manassas, however, Meagher's forces had been reduced by one thousand casualties. At Antietam, on September 17, the brigade was cited repeatedly in dispatches but, out of the remains of four regiments engaged, only about five hundred men survived it fit for duty.

At this point John O'Neill's 116th Pennsylvania Volunteers, commanded by Colonel Dennis Heenan and containing, as someone wrote, "mostly Irishmen and those from Cork to Donegal," joined Meagher's forces along with the 28th Massachusetts, largely Irish in makeup. Meagher's brigade formed 1 of 3 in Brigadier General Winfield Scott Hancock's First Division, II Corps, Right Grand Division, under the overall command of Major General Edwin V. Sumner.

The Battle of Fredericksburg on December 13, 1862, not only was the apex of the Irish Brigade's history, but also became a near-fatal turning point for Buckey O'Neill's father. Sumner sent the brigade against the Confederate stronghold on Marye's

Heights and Meagher's men charged gallantly into the rebel positions six times, strewing the slopes of the bastion with dead and wounded, the sprigs of green stuck in their caps a melancholy touch among the dead and dying. Captain O'Neill fell gravely wounded as a ball penetrated his right shoulder, causing partial paralysis and, as his casualty report later said, "disease of the heart and lungs."

Lieutenant Colonel St. Clair A. Mulholland (later breveted major general), second in command of the 116th Regiment, described Captain O'Neill's ordeal: "Captain O'Neill was shot through the right lung, the ball making a terrible wound from which he never fully recovered, and finally causing his death . . . the wound at Fredericksburg was his third."

Confederate General James Longstreet described the Irish charges on Marye's Heights as "the bravest action of the war," but Meagher's brigade suffered for its valor. Of the 1,200 men who fought the battle, only about 300 stood muster next day.

John O'Neill, whose wound was believed mortal, and who actually was listed as "killed in action" in preliminary reports, clung to life and began his agonizing recovery in a Washington hospital. He was only twenty-eight and had a tenacious will to live. In April, 1863, he received his discharge and the following September was appointed, by letter from Secretary of War Edwin Stanton, a captain in the Invalid Corps. During the latter days of the war, according to one source, he served as provost marshal for the District of Columbia and as a member of the military commission for the seven southwestern counties of Virginia. He became a member of the Union Veteran's League, the GAR, Loyal Legion, Odd Fellows Order, and Masonic Order (thirty-second degree), and at the end of his life was serving as a clerk in the Treasury Department.

In the years following the war, the captain's family grew to four healthy children: William, the oldest; John Bernard; Eugene Brady; and, the youngest, Mary Henning. William attended public schools in Washington and learned typesetting and legal shorthand along the way. In 1880, a U.S. Census taker [in Phoenix] listed William O. O'Neill's profession as "lawyer," but there is no evidence that he had obtained a law degree in the usual sense. His knowledge of court reporting might have been loosely translated to "lawyer," but it appears that he was a lawyer by profession only in the sense that he sometimes professed to be one.

By age nineteen he was eager to quit Washington, D.C., and find a high road to some place he had not yet been, preferably one with plenty of elbow room, opportunity, and adventure. Such a place was propitiously mentioned in the spring of 1879, when a news item appeared in the *Washington Star* under the heading EMIGRATION FROM WASHINGTON. The item read, "A number of gentlemen are about forming a company here for the purpose of emigrating to and settling in Arizona Territory, and it is proposed if possible to start with about 100 men pledged to aid and assist each other, and on arriving in the Territory to take up some of the public domain."

For young O'Neill, Washington held little in the way of allurement. While the Irish American of the nineteenth century was not much in the way of a frontiersman (being apt to think of the West largely in terms of Indian, desert, and fever), Arizona Territory had an enthralling ring to it. He remembered the newspaper stories that had appeared just a year earlier, relating how the great "Pathfinder" John C. Frémont had gone, with appointment by President Hayes, to take over the governorship of the wild stretch of land and how Frémont had waxed eloquent in print over Arizona's endless potential for the ambitious, hard-working, young man. William recalled clearly, too, the news of the great silver strike in the Territory in 1877. The event had filled newspaper columns with breathless stories of instant riches, wild and untrammeled mountains and Indian-haunted deserts, towns springing up overnight, fortunes won and lost, grizzled prospectors, mountain men, cattlemen, and lawmen—intrepid all.

On March 15, 1879, O'Neill wrote a carefully phrased letter to the secretary for Arizona Territory in Tucson, stretching the

truth a bit in the first few words, but seriously determined nonetheless: "I am a young lawyer, also a practical printer and am
desirous to reap whatever advantage that may accrue by taking
the advice of Horace Greeley and seeking a new home and
better fortune in the land of the setting sun. . . ."

The territorial government, eager to attract young professional men to Arizona, answered O'Neill's letter and encouraged
him. It is probable that they went so far as to line up a job for
the adventuresome young man—a job based on the second of
his self-proclaimed skills—and six months after writing of his
wish to follow Horace Greeley's advice, William Owen O'Neill
went west.

CHAPTER THREE

Stopover in Tombstone

DISAPPOINTED in the Vail's Rangers endeavor and perhaps tiring of the *Arizona Gazette* job and of Phoenix in general, O'Neill left the town in the fall of 1880. He headed southwest and crossed the San Pedro, following the silver scent that had drawn thousands of fortune hunters to a town founded only a year previously and, with a keen sense of the macabre, named Tombstone.

As a newspaperman, and particularly as a saloon habitué, Buckey knew something about Tombstone before he ever decided to pull up his shallow stakes in Phoenix to ride down to the notorious mining camp. Everybody knew about Tombstone, and nowhere was it better advertised than in the saloons and gambling parlors. In those places grubby prospectors, tongues oiled, spun fantastic tales of silver mines named "Lucky Cuss" and "Tough Nut," with streaks so pure you could push a double eagle against them and leave an impression clean as a die.

To Buckey, Tombstone epitomized the "real West" as only an Eastern tenderfoot could visualize it; to most others, the town was a boil on the territorial backside, an evil eruption, growing bigger and more uncontrollable—"coming to a head" in the nastiest sense of the phrase—with each passing day.

A dreamy, gray-eyed miner named Ed Shieffelin held responsibility for the town and its memorably gruesome name. Shieffelin, who had prospected in seven Western states and who would test the Klondike some years later, had found rich ledges of silver in the hills flanking the San Pedro Valley in the summer of 1877. Shieffelin's strike, which a Tucson assayer valued at $15,000 per ton of ore, opened a stampede of such proportions that in three years the miner's tents and shacks at the foot of the diggings had blossomed into a town of some 500 buildings (2 of them housing newspapers) and a population of more than 3,500. Metal production in the Territory in 1880 jumped to 5 times that of 10 years previously—from $800,000 to $4,000,000.

Shieffelin's initial mine and subsequently the town were named by their founder who recalled asking a soldier what he might find out in the blistering-hot Dragoon Mountain country. The reply was "Your tombstone."

Tombstone, at the time Buckey O'Neill decided to look at it, was described in the *Prescott Democrat* in the orotund style of the day by one who had visited there and left with mixed feelings:

On a level ridge among the rolling hills and undulating plains, extending from the Dragoon range on the north to the Mule Mountains on the south, and about nine miles from the San Pedro River, is the city of Tombstone. . . . To the north, sixteen miles away, the Dragoon Mountains, the former stronghold of the Apache Chief Cochise—rear their rocky and rugged outlines, while the low range of the Whetstones on the west and the massive chain of the Huachucas on the south afford a pleasant relief from the base and barren hills and sunscorched plains which make up the foreground of the picture and encircle the city of silver-bearing renown all round about.

The writer also felt constrained to speak of the "living tide of moving humanity; a surging sea of hurrying, crowding, jostling human beings who line the sidewalks and fill the streets at all hours of the day." And, observing the constant babble about silver, new strikes, assay figures, and money won and lost at the gaming tables, the *Democrat* piece concluded, " . . . Mammon has here set up his altar, and thousands daily and nightly worship assiduously at his shrine."

Buckey spent a day or two leaning on his meager savings, distinctly un-Mammon-like, and getting a feel of the town. Tombstone definitely could be felt. Almost every road and path, particularly the well-traveled Fremont Street, were covered with several inches of a lime-like powder that stirred in low clouds at the slightest movement, clinging to boot and trouser leg. This fine dust blew skyward in the breeze or in the swirl of hooves and wheels, in enormous stifling and blinding clouds.

There also was a feeling of sullenness about many of the idlers on Tombstone's calcined board walks: the leaners against storefronts, the flow of horsemen trailing clouds of the pumice-fine dust behind them as they wandered in and out of town and through the bat-wing saloon doors. In a measure, this forbidding atmosphere later was offset by the artificial gaiety of such places as the Oriental, the Tombstone Saloon, the Crystal Palace, and in the town's famous Birdcage Theater that presented vaudeville acts and dramatic productions. In such places a man could wash from his mouth the lime dust of Tombstone's streets. The water wouldn't do it; piped in from the Dragoons, it had an iron-sour tang that boosted bar sales and, some said, made the most determined of teetotalers turn to the hard stuff.

Tombstone also had a Shakespeare Circle, a Terpsichorean Club, 4 churches, some 60 lawyers, and a volunteer fire department. The latter organization would be put to its severest test in June, 1881, when a whiskey barrel exploded and started a fire that ultimately burned 66 buildings and consumed $175,-000 in property.

Before he found his way to the office of Tombstone's most famous newspaper, the *Epitaph*, Buckey found time to check on the Mammon altars—the faro layouts—in the town's gambling parlors and to meet some of their more notable and notorious habitués. The largest, gaudiest, and busiest of the saloons was the Oriental on Fifth and Allen streets. Tombstone's deputy marshal, Wyatt Earp, owned an interest in the Oriental, whose barkeep was a steely blue-eyed man with flowing chestnut-colored hair and a handle-bar moustache. His name was Nashville Franklin Leslie, best known as "Buckskin Frank." Among the Oriental's faro dealers at the time of Buckey's visits were Luke Short and William Barclay "Bat" Masterson, the latter having come to town at about the same time as Buckey himself. Both Short and Masterson were hired to protect the Oriental from trouble as well as to deal cards, and Short recently had

fulfilled the former obligation by shooting a troublemaker
named Charlie Storms. Tombstone's newspapers covered such
events with almost ludicrous piety, but some wag generally
managed to inject a bit of black humor into the shootouts. In
the case of Short's termination of Charlie Storms, an epitaph
was suggested for the dead man that went:

> He had sand in his craw
> But he was slow on the draw,
> So we laid him under the daisies.

Other notables in and out of town at various times were John
H. "Doc" Holliday, "Big Nose Kate" Elder, a gambler named
"Johnny-Behind-the-Deuce," Curley Bill Brocius, and Johnny
Ringo.

Buckey's brief venture in Tombstone-style journalism was
with the *Epitaph*, founded, owned, and operated by John Clum,
Tombstone's mayor and late Indian agent on the San Carlos
Apache Reservation. Buckey found the *Epitaph* office in an
adobe building on Fremont Street, between Third and Fourth,
and went to work there as a reporter almost as quickly as he
had hired on as typesetter in Phoenix.

Clum, previously the owner of the *Tucson Citizen*, had moved
to Tombstone the previous spring. From San Francisco he
ordered a Washington hand press, type cases, and supplies and
set up business in a twenty by forty-foot canvas-covered shed.
After hiring two itinerant printers, Clum and his men worked
in daylight and by kerosene lamp at night to bring out the first
issue of the paper on May 1, 1880. From the start it was an influential force in the town, fearlessly backing the peace efforts
of Deputy Marshal Wyatt Earp and the brothers Earp—Virgil,
Wyatt's chief of police, and Morgan, who served under Virgil
as special officer.

Arizona's *preux chevalier*, Buckey O'Neill became, in the
words of one of Tombstone's historians, "a lesser figure of Tombstone's fourth estate." He quickly got up to his ears in the fac-
tionalization that was splitting the town down the middle,

marking a path that led directly to the O.K. Corral, just across the street from the *Epitaph* office.

Tombstone, in fact, had much to offer the lawbreaker; it attracted stage robbers, cattle rustlers, con artists, murderers and waylayers like a lodestone. The town was isolated and insulated from the law: "For isolation," one authority said, "it was as good as the Big Bend Country, and it did not have the drawback offered by the Texas Rangers." Furthermore, it was within easy riding distance of such notorious gang hideaways as Galeyville and Charleston, where nests of "cow boys," as the southeastern Arizona badmen were called, enjoyed virtual immunity from the badge.

The *Epitaph* carried no bylines in 1880, so there is no chance to examine Buckey's personal contributions to the paper, but it is likely that he stuck around long enough to observe and help chronicle the rush of events that was leading the Earp brothers into a confrontation with the Clanton gang. Unfortunately, it also appears likely that he left Tombstone before the actual climax of the feud.

N. H. "Old Man" Clanton, headquartered in a ranch near Charleston, eight miles west of Tombstone, had been booted out of both Texas and California for cattle rustling. He and his sons Ike, Phin, and Billy, as well as Tom and Frank McLowery, Johnny Ringo, and various other guns-for-hire, were believed to be preying on bullion shipments from Tombstone. Wells-Fargo had hired Wyatt Earp as an undercover agent to protect its stage shipments, and Earp in turn deputized brothers Virgil and Morgan, Bat Masterson, Doc Holliday, Buckskin Frank Leslie, and others to track down the stage bandits.

Buckey probably helped write up the March 15, 1881, robbery of the Bisbee stage by the Curly Bill Brocius gang and the subsequent wild-goose chase by the Earps through the Dragoon Mountains. The Bisbee stage holdup widened the Earp-Clanton feud and Buckey's paper, the *Epitaph*, got right in the middle of it, supporting the Earp "Law and Order League." On the other

hand, Clum's competitor, the *Nugget*, just across Fremont
Street from the *Epitaph*, openly sided with the "cow boys,"
Clanton, Brocius, and their followers.

The meeting between the Earp brothers (with Doc Holliday)
and the Clanton gang (with Frank and Tom McLowery), took
place on October 26, 1881. After thirty seconds of desperate
battle in the O.K. Corral, three of the Clanton faction lay dead,
two of the Earp brothers wounded. The *Epitaph's* coverage of
the shoot-out was full and sanctimoniously detailed, as were
accounts in the rival *Nugget* and newspapers throughout the
Territory.

In all likelihood, Buckey read of the engagement from afar.

CHAPTER FOUR

A Wandering Interlude

 OF THE SEVERAL GAPS in the early Arizona career of Buckey O'Neill, none gapes wider and offers more puzzlement than the months between the spring (or summer) of 1881, when he left Tombstone, and the spring of 1882, when he reached the territorial capital at Prescott. In all there is a hiatus of almost a year, devoid of any real documentation in either O'Neill's own words or in those of his friends, contemporaries, and chroniclers.

For a man with a fairly full-bloomed ego, and for one who could write well, Buckey was never much in the way of memoir-keeper or diarist. When he first came to Arizona, he was too young and undecided to worry about such things, and later on he kept too frenetically busy—and was still too young —to ponder his place in history or to collect his experiences and day-to-day encounters for a future memoir.

Thus the duration of his stay in Tombstone (and, for that matter, what precisely he saw and did there) is unknown. Moreover, it is not known exactly where he went after leaving. Two suggestions crop up regularly in the occasional writings about O'Neill, attempting to fill this exasperating gap: Hawaii and New Mexico.

Buckey O'Neill in Hawaii is an enticing will-o'-the-wisp notion but unfortunately is little more than that. One O'Neill fan, Ralph Keithley, makes the claim that Buckey visited the islands some time in 1881, when "the charms of Hawaii were the real McCoy." Inexplicably, Keithley says Buckey didn't like his sojourn there ("It took all the steam right out of his soul and slowed him down to a walk."). The writer claims O'Neill returned to the mainland after only two weeks, to tramp about in Southern California.

Unquestionably, Buckey's youthful wanderlust and adventure-seeking could have drawn him to Hawaii, but it seems unlikely he would have returned, his soul steamless or not, in so short a time. Surely Hawaii, a foreign country to Americans in 1881, would have been as alluring, if not more so, as Arizona Territory to a footloose twenty-one-year-old.

Sometime in mid-1881, Buckey did spend a few months in New Mexico. From the territorial capital at Santa Fe he made his way to Albuquerque, where he found a short-time job as court stenographer for the Second Judicial District. An acquaintance, Bernard S. Rodey, later a judge, wrote that Buckey established a reputation in Albuquerque—as he had in Phoenix and Tombstone—as a daring gambler in off-courtroom hours. "Now O'Neill was never a recluse," Judge Rodey wrote, "and while not immoral in any gross sense, would never have succeeded as a monk, and as gambling surrounded everybody and everything in those days, like the cannon at Balaklava, he naturally bucked about everything in the shape of a game of chance that his leisure, his luck or his salary permitted."

Early in the spring of 1882, Buckey returned to Phoenix and for a few weeks scouted around for work and renewed acquaintances. He worked briefly as special deputy again for Marshal Henry Garfias and had his inevitable encounter with the kind of police work Garfias butted heads with daily.

In June, 1882, three cowboys—William Hardy and Frank and John Lile—rode into Phoenix drunk, firing their six-guns in the air along Washington Street and making a generally obscene nuisance of themselves. After stopping off at various saloons to hoist a few quick drinks, Hardy, pistol in hand, tried to ride his horse through the bat-wing doors of the Tiger Saloon. He banged his head against a hanging chandelier and fired several shots into the bar's ceiling, then rode back out, cursing and lurching down the street.

The activities of the loud-mouthed trio were duly reported to the marshal. Garfias, with special deputies O'Neill and High McDonald and another officer, ran down the drunken cowboys on a side street. Hardy cried to the others, "Boys, here they come! Let's meet 'em!" then charged insanely toward Garfias and his deputies, screaming "Come on, you sons of bitches!" Hardy fired a hasty shot at Garfias, who calmly dismounted, took aim, and hit Hardy in the pistol hand, then fired a second shot that blew the careening cowboy off his saddle.

Buckey, McDonald, and their partner joined Garfias in running down the two remaining waddies, who were captured without a fight and taken to jail. Hardy died that evening.

At a coroner's inquest, Buckey and Garfias testified as to the facts in the case and the verdict was rendered that Hardy "came to his death by pistol shots fired by the city marshal and posse, while attempting to arrest said deceased, and that we consider the act justifiable, the said deceased being in the act of resisting arrest."

Buckey considered his baptism of fire exciting enough but not nearly as exciting as the prospect of moving on. He had been in the Territory, after all, more than two years—minus a few months of unsatisfactory wandering in other places—and he had yet to see the great Arizona capital he had read so much about. The *Phoenix Gazette* recently had made a poetic tribute about Prescott that ran:

Ever has she been remarked as the "toniest" of the Territorial towns. Situated amid the pines that continually sing to her the saddest yet sweetest songs of nature, nestled among the hills at an elevation so high as to never permit the atmosphere to reach that temperature that makes us lose the starch in our garments as well as the polishing points in our manners and habits, she seems to gather refinement from her surroundings. The true indication of culture—not with an "ah" termination, as in its too, too Boston sense—seems to pervade her streets and permeate her homes. You can see more dignified and courtly gentlemen, stylish and polished young men, fascinating and elegant ladies in Prescott in a day, than in any other town of the same size your correspondent has ever visited.

With such a glowing endorsement from his former employer, and with nothing to hold him back, Buckey set out for Prescott, a town destined to be his home for sixteen years.

CHAPTER FIVE

A New Customer on Whiskey Row

PRESCOTT, a cool, high town up in the northwest central part of the Territory, was the first
and third territorial capital. In 1864, it became
the first (discounting the few months that the government had
been located in the Chino Valley, about eighteen miles to the
north). Then after bitterly relinquishing the honor three years
later to Tucson, it gladly took it back a decade later, in 1877.[2]

Hemmed in on three sides by great forest-shrouded slopes
rising to Spruce and Granite mountains and what later became
Mount Tritle, Prescott took its name from William Hickling
Prescott, "in honor of the eminent American writer and standard authority on Aztec and Spanish-American history." The
name apparently was the inspiration of Richard McCormick,
first secretary of the Territory and founder of the town's original
newspaper, the *Arizona Miner*. Streets in Prescott were named
for persons prominent in Arizona and Mexican history: Montezuma, Cortez, Coronado, Alarcón, Leroux, Walker, Goodwin,
and Gurley.

At the time Buckey O'Neill settled there, Prescott had a
population of about 5,000, including a large number of miners.
The area was rich in mining properties and prospects. One
authority predicted the Prescott environs would record an
astonishing 7,300 gold-mining claims before the strikes began
playing out.

As an experienced, if slightly itinerant, newspaperman with
background as typesetter, reporter, and editor on such frontier
journals as the *Phoenix Herald, Arizona Gazette,* and *Tomb-*

---

[2] Prescott lost the capital again, permanently, in 1889 to Phoenix.

stone Epitaph, Buckey had no trouble in his job-seeking in the capital. For the third time in as many Arizona towns, he turned to journalism for immediate practicality and as a fulcrum for other ventures.

In March, 1882, Buckey took a job with the *Arizona Miner*, the daily with Republican Party leanings. The paper was owned and edited by Charles Beach, a controversial if benign looking man who had trod the toes of his political and business opponents in the Territory since 1864. Besides being a newspaperman, Beach was a cattle dealer, contractor, railroad speculator, and magnet for trouble. A volunteer veteran of the Civil War battles of Glorieta and Valverde in New Mexico, Beach was to sell the *Miner* the year after Buckey came to work for him, but the two were to meet again that next year—under quite extraordinary circumstances.

Meantime, as Buckey joined the *Miner's* little staff, Beach and his paper were joined in the aftermath of another battle over the territorial governorship, a perpetual issue in Arizona politics of the prestatehood era, when governors came and went with irritating transience.[3] In the case of the unlamented John Charles Frémont, it was more "went" than "came," but Frémont's charade of a governorship had ended the previous October.

In March, 1880, Frémont had begun another of his extended junkets in the east, this time staying out of Arizona seven months. He returned two months before the convening of the Eleventh Legislative Assembly (which created the counties of Gila, Cochise, and Graham and incorporated the towns of Phoenix, Tombstone, and Prescott); then, in the summer of 1881, the absentee governor left again. This seemingly blatant disregard for his duties outraged Acting Governor John J. Gosper to the point that he submitted an official report to the secretary of the interior, administrator of all U.S. territories, strongly recommending that Frémont either be required to re-

---

[3] In Arizona's forty-eight years as a territory (1864–1912), it had a total of seventeen governors, serving an average of 2.8 years.

turn to attend to Arizona business or that he be asked to resign.

Gosper, a handsome, one-legged Union Army veteran, peti-
tioned both Presidents Garfield and Chester A. Arthur for the
governorship for himself and, when Frémont belatedly resigned
on October 11, 1881, Gosper claimed to have the support of
twelve of the Territory's sixteen newspapers, with only Charlie
Beach's *Arizona Miner* opposing him.

Beach, on hearing of the acting governor's claim, took the
opportunity to kindle a new fire under his long-simmering feud
with Gosper. Beach wrote that only Gosper's own paper, the
Phoenix Herald (which had given Buckey O'Neill his first job
in the Territory) was zealously backing its part owner. Beach
further claimed Gosper was nearly illiterate and a brazen op-
portunist, hinting that some kind of marital scandal, as well as
other skeletons, could be found in Gosper's closet. Beach flatly
predicted Gosper would never sit in the Governor's chair as
anything other than the *acting* chief executive.

Beach was quite correct in the latter prediction, for despite
Gosper's energetic campaign, President Arthur named a Penn-
sylvanian, Frederick A. Tritle, to the governorship on March
8, 1882. Tritle was not Beach's choice, but the nomination of
anyone but Gosper was inclined to please him.

Buckey O'Neill the gambler and saloon man was in no way
thwarted in these after-hours endeavors by becoming a resident
of Prescott. Besides having the distinction of being the seat of
the territorial government, the town had yet another allurement, succinctly described by a visitor in Buckey's own time.
"Prescott," the seemingly pleased tourist had said, "is a saloon
town and a whiskey town. It is also a faro town and a craps
town."

Most of the whiskey, faro, and craps could be found in the
establishments along Montezuma Street, between Gurley and
Goodwin, a section known throughout the Territory as "Whiskey Row." Here were located not only Prescott's Chinatown
(down along the banks of Granite Creek) but also such saloons

as Dan Thorn's, the Little Diana, the Arizona Brewery and Saloon, the Pacific Brewery, the Pine Tree, Cavanaugh's, the Nifty, Palace Bar, Union, Cobweb Hall, the Antler, and the Sazerac,[4] to name a few.

As in his brief tenures in Phoenix, Tombstone, and Albuquerque, Buckey's natural conviviality, his "take-my-bet-and-the-hell-with-it" attitude, his youthful vigor, exuberance, and wit, made him a star attraction along Whiskey Row. This natural affinity for the horny-handed scrabbling miner and workman, the grassroots, salt-of-the-earth types who found in the saloon some of the few pleasures in a life of sweat and back aches, was to give Buckey a dimension not found in the average politician and public man of the day. It was a facet of his character that acted in his behalf as a vote-getter and leader of men. Although his political opponents would try often to use his intimate knowledge of Whiskey Row and its denizens against him, such sanctimony always backfired. To its newest customer, Whiskey Row, while not exactly a *way* of life, was a *part* of life and an enjoyable part at that.

In July, 1882, Buckey took a brief two-day tour of duty in Globe, east of Phoenix, as court reporter to circuit judge D. H. Pinney, newly arrived in the Territory from Lockport, Illinois. For Buckey, it wasn't a particularly eventful two days except that when the session ended, Judge Pinney apparently offered his stenographer seventy-five dollars in fees and Buckey insisted on the full six-month stipend of five hundred dollars, claiming he had signed on for that period and was ready to work for Pinney until the end of the year. The judge refused to sign a warrant for the full stipend and Buckey refused to accept the seventy-five dollars. The rift with Judge Pinney was to have later repercussions.

The *Miner* reporting job offered its interesting moments and served to educate Buckey further in the burdensome problems of territorial politics. The new governor, Frederick Tritle, in

4 No one knew what "Sazerac" meant, but it was believed to be a New Orleans brandy.

his address to the Twelfth Legislative Assembly in January, 1883, revealed (unlike the addresses of his predecessor) a great deal of homework. Tritle expressed a natural interest in promoting Arizona's mining resources—he had been in Arizona only a few years attempting to develop the mining area around Jerome, and had a personal interest in the Comstock Lode in Nevada. He urged protection of the Territory's great forest reserves, drilling of artesian wells, and the stocking of streams and lakes for the sportsman, and spoke alarmingly of what he rightly considered the two greatest problems of Arizona—Indian depredations and lawlessness.

On the latter point, the plague of killings, stage banditry, cattle rustling, and general hell-raising had reached such staggering proportions the previous spring that President Arthur threatened to place Arizona under martial law unless law and order were reestablished quickly, particularly in Cochise County. The declaration obviously was directed at the happenings in Tombstone that were erupting while Buckey was employed on the *Epitaph*.

While pursuing copy for the *Miner* and keeping an eye peeled on what was happening in the rest of Arizona, Buckey was informed in September, 1883, that M. V. Howard, stenographer in Prescott's Third Judicial District Court, had resigned. Buckey, who had served in that capacity in Albuquerque and for two days in Globe, asked for and got the job.

For two months it was routine.

CHAPTER SIX

The Bloodiest Day in Court

THERE IS SOMETHING bizarre in the timing of Buckey's seemingly innocuous job as court reporter in the Third District Court. A thousand circumstances could have dictated a course different from what was to follow: he might have been out of town, or not interested, when the vacancy opened up; he might not have been selected for it; Mr. Howard could have decided to stay on a few months longer. But the fact is that Buckey took the job in September and something like seventy days later was at his post when one of the most violent and bloody episodes in American judicial history occurred.

On the face of it, the case opening that December 1 was a bore. The issue was water rights in the Kirkland Valley, some twenty-five miles southwest of Prescott. The plaintiff was a cordial widow, a Mrs. Kelsey, who owned a ranch in the valley adjoining that of Patrick McAteer, the defendant in the case. Mrs. Kelsey was suing for the right to use one-half of the waters of Kirkland Creek, which flowed past both the Kelsey and McAteer properties.

Although such cases were commonplace, they were important, since the life or death of a ranch or farm often depended on securing water rights; but the hearings were filled with dull legalities and, usually, dull litigants.

In the case of Kelsey vs. McAteer, however, there were features that could not show in the docketbook or the legal brief. The case seethed with pent-up emotion and the principal emotion was hatred.

The suit had been pending for five years and during this time, certain lines had been drawn—specifically, between the defendent, Patrick McAteer, and Charles W. Beach, Buckey O'Neill's boss for a short time on the *Miner* who seemed to have a tragic affinity for violence. Beach was the son-in-law of Mrs. Kelsey, the plaintiff, and, as one newspaper delicately described it, "managed her interests outside of counsel." As will be seen, Beach's role in the case went beyond that of a dutiful son-in-law.

McAteer was a brooding, forbidding man who had built a dark reputation in Prescott with his smoldering, ungovernable temper. A bad man when aroused, McAteer's open enmity toward Beach had caused friends of the former newspaper owner to warn him that his life might be in danger. Beach, although scoffing at such an idea, took to carrying a revolver.

On the third day of the trial, Saturday, December 3, 1883, the Third District Courtroom began to fill early. Kirkland Valley people were keenly interested in the case. Among the onlookers was "Uncle Jimmy" More, who owned land along the contested creek and who knew both Mrs. Kelsey and McAteer. Also in the spectator section was Charlie Beach. McAteer arrived with his counsel, District Attorney Charles B. Rush and Rush's partner, J. C. Herndon; Mrs. Kelsey with her lawyer, Attorney General Clark Churchill, and his secretary, George Tinker. Hearing the case was the chief justice of the Territorial Supreme Court, C. G. W. French, with William O. O'Neill taking down the testimony.

An early witness that morning was one Moses Langley, a Kirkland Valley man who testified for Mrs. Kelsey. It was during the cross-examination of Langley that all hell broke loose. Langley was being sternly examined by Rush when Churchill rose and objected to the line of questioning. In a few seconds, despite Justice French's attempt to gavel for order, the two lawyers were in a crimson-faced screaming argument, at the peak of which Churchill shouted the word which, like some malevolent theatrical cue, turned the courtroom into a battlefield: "LIAR!"

It was like touching a hair-trigger. Rush, already livid with rage, picked up a heavy inkstand, hurling it at Churchill as he vaulted the table separating him from the attorney general, and grabbed Churchill by the throat.

Pandemonium ensued. Probably in less than a minute, the courtroom was reduced to a bloody shambles.

As Rush seized Churchill in a death grip, the prosecutor's assistant, J. C. Herndon, rose from his chair and struck Churchill from behind. Buckey O'Neill, watching the incredible attack from his station below the dumbfounded, gavel-pounding Justice French's bench, leaped to his feet as Churchill began to falter under the throttling and pummeling by Rush and Herndon. Churchill's helper, George Tinker, joined Buckey, dodging the flying chairs, inkwells, and cuspidors.

Patrick McAteer, totally unhinged, sprang from his chair, drew an enormous double-bladed knife, and waded into the crowd at the front of the spectators' section. He moved directly toward Uncle Jimmy More, who screamed piteously, "Mac, for God's sake, don't cut me!" McAteer wasn't listening. He lunged at More and drove the knife to its hilt into the old man's left arm. The blade penetrated past the bone, severed an artery, and sank into More's chest. McAteer pulled the blade free. As the shrieking More, his arm pumping gouts of blood, stumbled toward the door, his now completely mad assailant turned toward Charlie Beach.

Perhaps ten seconds had passed. Beach, standing, saw the attack on More. As McAteer lurched toward him, slashing at another spectator on the way, Beach managed to dodge the knife blow. The blade hacked the left side of his neck, missing the jugular vein by less than an inch. The force of the blow knocked Beach over the railing dividing the auditorium from the bar. As he fell, McAteer banged through the gate of the railing and strode toward Buckey O'Neill.

Buckey and George Tinker, with a few well-aimed punches, had succeeded in disengaging Rush and Herndon from Clark Churchill and were holding the two partners off the crumpled

attorney general when McAteer saw them. Buckey leaped backward as McAteer lunged but, even so, the knife slashed painfully between the first two fingers of his left hand. As Buckey
shoved McAteer away from him, he caught a glimpse of Charlie
Beach, moving toward McAteer.

Beach had picked himself up from the foot of the railing and
felt his neck wound. Though it was pouring blood, the gash was
not deep. As McAteer, the bloody knife still in his hand,
stumbled backward from Buckey O'Neill's shove, Beach drew
a .38-caliber Colt revolver from a pocket, took split-second aim
at McAteer's back, and pulled the trigger.

The gun's roar in the small, closed courtroom was like a
cannon shot. The bullet struck McAteer on an angle under the
left shoulder blade, felling the madman like a pole-axed ox at
Buckey's feet. Buckey instinctively reached down and freed the
blood-stained knife from McAteer's grip.

The roar of the Colt had brought a sudden end to the wild
slugfest. The courtroom was like an abattoir hit by a tornado.
Splinters of chairs, benches, and tables strewn about on the
floor and the piles of legal paperwork were covered with blood;
the floor of the courtroom was slippery with it, the stairs leading from the outside were splotched with it, shirts were soaked
in a mixture of blood and ink. One fear-stricken onlooker fled
into the street shouting "Everybody's dead! They're killing each
other like sheep up there!"

McAteer's first victim, Jimmy More, meantime had staggered
outside and made his way to Dr. Kendall's Drugstore near the
courthouse. There he fainted and was hurriedly taken to the
nearby St. Joseph's Hospital.

McAteer himself was taken to the boarding house where he
had roomed during the trial. The examining doctor said bluntly
that nothing could save him. Beach's bullet had lodged an inch
and a half deep and about four inches to the right of the spine.
McAteer's extremities were cold and he complained of pain
in his bowels, indications, the doctor said, that the bullet had
struck the spinal cord as it plowed across the back.

Beach and Buckey, Churchill, and the innocent spectator were treated, bandaged, and released.

McAteer almost fooled the doctors but not quite. He lived to see the opening of 1884 but died, one month and a day after his rampage.

Jimmy More, two weeks after his wound, gave up his infected arm to the surgeon to save his life. He lived an otherwise full life, dying of natural causes in 1903.

Beach, exonerated by a grand jury of the shooting of Mc-Ateer, could never keep out of trouble thereafter. Following the courtroom fray he resumed ownership of the *Miner* and dabbled in the cattle business. The *Prescott Courier*, his archrival, expressed its editorial policy without restraint a few days after the McAteer shooting, saying Beach had "furnished an excuse for shooting McAteer . . . he had done it to save the life of W. L. 'Bucky' O'Neil [*sic*] whom he claimed had been pushed into a corner at knifepoint by McAteer." The *Courier* then continued:

The Courier, as its readers know, has always avoided taking sides in local or law squabbles. It has known, from the first, that McAteer was right and Beach was wrong on the water question, and we do not hesitate to state that Beach has for years, invited other people to bring suits against McAteer. . . . McAteer's friends believe that this disgraceful murderous affair was planned by Beach, Churchill and Co. Beach was observed to be very uneasy in court, and to have touched Churchill with his elbow. The fact of his being in the town in which he lives and in one of its most sacred places, with a loaded pistol in his pocket, goes to show that his mind was intent on murder.

Two years later Beach purchased all rights, title, and interest to the McAteer ranch in Kirkland Valley. The property was described as "one of the finest properties in Yavapai County," but the new owner did not live long to enjoy his final victory. In 1889, as Beach sat alone in his room at Mrs. Taylor's boarding house in Prescott, writing a letter to his son in Los Angeles, a man named George W. Young aimed a double-barreled shotgun through Beach's window and pulled both triggers. The blast blew off half of Beach's head. Young later said Beach had alienated the affections of Mrs. Young.

Although the murder had no connection with the McAteer controversy, most saw Beach's death as bringing the case full circle.

Attorney General Churchill and District Attorney Rush were fined five hundred dollars each for "contempt of court," apparently the only legal charge handy but one scarcely doing justice to the bloodletting created by their temper outburst.

Neither was Justice French up to an adequate description of the bloody December 3. He called it simply "a lamentable occurrence."

CHAPTER SEVEN

Hoof and Horn *and a Dun*
for the Thieving Thirteenth

BUCKEY'S TRADEMARK was a brown paper roll-your-own. A fully committed fag addict, he was seldom seen without the stub of a cigarette in his mouth or on its way to replace the Bull Durham "makins" dangling from his teeth as he deftly rolled and twisted his "nail" with unerring precision. A never-ending supply of tobacco and paper seemed to flow from his shirt pocket but the third most essential ingredient invariably was missing. His close friend, Jim McClintock, claimed that Buckey's commonest greeting was "Hi, Jim, gimme a match." The affable McClintock said he seemed to spend most of his time, when in Buckey's presence, digging for wooden lucifers to keep his friend's chain of butts alight.

Smoking, like a daily drop-in at Cavanaugh's or the Sazerac on Whiskey Row, was a part of the O'Neill routine of burning off nervous energy. A fundamental part of Buckey's makeup was an absolute inability to remain still if hours remained in the day. Even with his feet propped on his desk at the *Miner* office or on the rail at a favorite Row establishment, his mind raced with ideas—books he had read, political philosophies being absorbed, events in the Territory and the nation. Now twenty-four, with five years in Arizona behind him, an undefined but seemingly bright future ahead, roots at last planted in Prescott, Buckey's character was maturing. Its outstanding feature was ambition.

Buckey considered court reporting and, for that matter, working on somebody else's newspaper to be stopgap employment.

Not long before the unforgettable December 3 courtroom brawl, he was elevated to the editorship of the *Miner* and held the job until February, 1884, presumably relinquishing it when Charlie Beach returned as owner-editor. Whatever the case, Buckey's leave-taking apparently was cordial; the *Miner* was to become a staunch friend and ally, which watched with pleasure the upswinging career of its former editor.

Buckey had a plan for his own newspaper. It was not to be the ordinary desert variety of weekly—or even daily—that was proliferating and dying with stunning regularity all over the Territory. With the cattle industry growing—an estimated 625,000 head in Arizona in 1884—Buckey's idea was to specialize, giving cattlemen their own journal. It would provide the cattlemen a medium for advertising cattle brands, buying and selling, and keeping abreast of the industry in both Arizona and neighboring cattle country. And it would serve as a soapbox from which to call for battle against the cowman's number one nemesis—in the 1880's, worse than disease and drought—the rustler.

Ordering his equipment from Phoenix, Buckey was able to launch his paper, *Hoof and Horn*, on July 30, 1885. It was an eight-page magazine-sized journal, ten by thirteen inches, ten cents a copy, boldly proclaiming to be "The only journal devoted exclusively to the Stockgrowing interests of Arizona."

The *Hoof and Horn* was never a gold mine. From the first it struggled for existence, despite Buckey's sprightly style and sense of innovation. He urged cattlemen to advertise their brands in its pages, then offered a reward of $100 for the capture of anyone stealing stock with brands registered in *Hoof and Horn*. Far more lucrative than the cattlemen's ads and copy sales, though, was the paper's official status with the Yavapai County government. Buckey had wangled the "official" imprimatur through courthouse cronies and thus was assured of a regular bundle of county legal advertising. Moreover, as a job printer, as well as newspaper publisher in the capital, territorial government printing came his way. Not many months after launching *Hoof and Horn*, he was able to present the Legislature with a thumping $6,500 printing bill.

At almost any other time, the territorial legislature would have gagged on such a debt, but the ultraliberal (especially in spending) Thirteenth Legislative Assembly, popularly called "the Thieving Thirteenth," paid it without a whimper. After all, what was $6,500 when the city of Phoenix was given $100,-000 for an insane asylum, Tempe an appropriation for a normal school, Tucson $25,000 to begin a university, Florence $12,000 for a bridge? The Legislature itself allowed $50,744 for its own operating expenses, a sum $46,744 in excess of what it was legally entitled to spend.

Buckey not only collected his printing bill but took a further step in dunning the legislature for the five hundred dollars in stenography fees he had failed to collect three years earlier in Globe. Judge Pinney's refusal to pay the six-month stipend and the Illinoisian's offer of seventy-five dollars for the two-day stint had never ceased to irk Buckey. Like the man carefully but unconsciously falsifying his income tax return, it seems never to have occurred to O'Neill that he might be wrong in gouging the government for services never rendered.

Buckey's argument that he had "signed on" for a full six-month term back in July, 1882, and that records would show he had received no payment whatever, seemed cogent to the Thirteenth Assembly and it paid the five-hundred-dollar fee by a special act, Number Fifty-Two, Laws of the Territory of Arizona.

Back in Lockport, Illinois, Judge Pinney somehow learned of Special Act Fifty-Two and fired off an outraged telegram to Governor Tritle calling the five-hundred-dollar payment to W. O. O'Neill "a first-class steal."

Judge Pinney soon would have a chance to repeat this charge —publicly.

Buckey O'Neill, left, Captain Valentine, and Jake Henkle of the Milligan Guards, later the Prescott Grays (Sharlot Hall Museum, Prescott).

CHAPTER EIGHT

Pauline and the Rubicon of Bachelorhood

BUCKEY O'NEILL, ever gregarious among men, exuding self-confidence and wit, lover of a good story to go with a convivial glass of whiskey, was red-faced and genteel in the presence of a lady. In his mid-twenties now, he was Prescott's preeminent bachelor, and was known to most of the town's unmarried womenfolk. Standing about an inch and a half under six feet, with mellow brown eyes, straight and close-cropped brown hair, a romantically dark complexion, well-shaped nose straight as an arrow from bridge to tip, rather sensuous lips surmounted by a trimmed and stylish moustache that curved silkily down from each nostril around and slightly below each corner of his mouth, Buckey was not just handsome, he was—to use the word in currency at the time—"dashing." And, sporting a white stetson, casual western-style wash trousers, plaid shirt, and scuffed boots, with his Bull Durham cigarette casually and perpetually smoldering, he was the quintessence of young and rugged Arizona manhood.

As a well-known Whiskey Row mainstay, gambler, and friend of many of Prescott's rough-shod miners, cattlemen, Chinese and ne'er-do-wells, there was a trace of the scandalous about him that, in the eyes of the ladies, was construed as an additional fillip of charm. Another was added when he joined Prescott's local militia group, the Milligan Guards—later called the "Grays"—and got to wear their spiffy uniform with its curved shoulderboards, brass-buttoned tunic, and brocaded cap.

In the fall of 1885, a traveling medicine show rolled into Prescott huckstering a miraculous cure-all called "Wizard Oil." Buckey, in attendance during one of the spieler's performances, saw for the first time a lovely young lady he later learned was the daughter of Captain Schindler. The captain was attached to the commissary office at Whipple Barracks, north of the capitol, then headquarters of the Military Department of Arizona. The lady's name, he learned, was Pauline; she was twenty and unmarried. Not long after the medicine show left town, Buckey arranged to be introduced to Miss Schindler at a band concert at Whipple. In later years Pauline recalled:

He was so nervous he almost dropped his white cowboy hat in the dust. It worried me nearly sick. I later discovered he was always like that when first meeting strangers, and very inclined to blush. That made him mad, which made him redder. Red cheeks and white hat were a contrast that night! But he rolled a cigarette and was very much at ease. Owen was lost without a cigarette.

To Pauline, with few exceptions, Buckey was "Owen"; she was the only person to use his middle name and probably used it for that very reason.

She had been born Pauline Marie on January 13, 1865, at the Presidio, San Francisco, daughter of W. F. R. and Rosalie Young Schindler, both natives of Germany. Schindler had served for several years as editor of the *San Francisco Post*, a German-language newspaper. He soon was to resign his army commission at Fort Bowie to become assistant editor of his new son-in-law's cattle journal, *Hoof and Horn*.

Buckey and Pauline's courtship was a classic whirlwind affair, about six months in duration. It was not long enough to prevent considerable tongue-clucking among the capital's society women but it was long enough for Buckey. On April 27, 1886, the couple was married at the Prescott Catholic Church with Father F. X. Guibitosi, S.J., officiating.

Buckey's militia outfit, the Prescott Grays, serenaded the newlyweds, champagne and cigars were passed around, and the two were escorted to their new home in West Prescott, an area jokingly called "Snob Hill," probably for Buckey's benefit since so few Whiskey Row notables lived there.

As a newspaper editor-proprietor, Buckey couldn't resist the temptation to make page-one news of his marriage. Later, as a candidate for political office, his good-humored announcement was held against him as flippant and disrespectful to the institution of holy matrimony and proof positive that he devoted far more time to gambling than to observing his marriage

Pauline Schindler O'Neill (Sharlot Hall Museum, Prescott).

vows. Such charges were not only stupid but also foolhardy. No one made political hay from Buckey's *Hoof and Horn* manifesto. It was exultant, exuberant, good-natured, quotable, and widely quoted—a frank and funny confession of a happily married man. He wrote:

MARRIED—O'Neill-Schindler—in Prescott, Arizona Territory, April 27, 1886, by the Reverend Guibitosi, William O. O'Neill to Miss Pauline M. Schindler.

By reference to the above notice it will be seen that the editor of 'Hoof and Horn' has passed the Rubicon of bachelorhood, and now rests in the Beulah land of matrimony. Do we like it? Go your bottom dollar on the proposition if you would realize a hundred per cent on your money. Sensations? Describe them? Impossible! Elysian, enchanting, divine, glorious, aesthetic, intense, entrancing, captivating, inspiring, ecstatic, seraphic, absorbing, engrossing, engulfing, monopolizing, engaging, attractive, magnetic—the vocabulary fails us. They are heavenly, with enough of the human thrown in, to enable them to double discount anything in the line of luxury that St. Peter turns

Buckey and Pauline's Prescott home (Sharlot Hall Museum).

the key on. The double-distilled joy that a man feels after putting an incurable kink in a fat faro bank—the wild elation that sometimes seizes the soul of the world-worn editor, when he has Sullivanized the man who wants an immediate retraction—are as nothing compared with them. They are yum-yum, long drawn out. The experience is like unto nothing, but the consumption of the soul by the ethereal flames of Promethean fires. No human institution compares with it, and when it fails don't deal us a hand in the game of life. To be born is only notable because it makes the experience possible; to die is only dreadful because it may terminate it. We have it bad; we know; but there is some satisfaction in knowing that the party of the second part has it worse. Have you tried it? Stay with it. If you haven't try it on at once. Only a lottery? Nonsense! It's the squarest kind of a game in which you 'put up' the cards for your own benefit, and win or lose on your own merits. Young man and old, get into the stream. If you can't take care of yourself after getting into it, get the right kind of a girl and she will see that your head doesn't get under water and at the same time teach you that there are some things in this life that border very nearly, if not within, the boundary of unalloyed bliss.

If the six-month courtship didn't start the social machinery tsk-tsking, Buckey's front page love letter did. And difficult as it must have been to draw evil implication from such "unalloyed bliss," Buckey's later political opponents would have no hesitation in extrapolating from it that Pauline's husband was a hard-drinking, gambling-drugged fiend of violent temper and vile language who crashed through the locked door of his house in the wee morning hours, stupified from his Whiskey Row orgies.

Pauline, though she doubtlessly worried about her husband's gambling proclivities as would any wife in charge of the domestic purse-strings, appears to have been a model of indulgence—a truly doting wife. If she and "Owen" had any serious marital problems, no one ever knew of them. Her few recorded recollections of her marriage to Buckey were invariably tender and loving.

In later years one of her favorite stories about him concerned how "He was so gentle and kind-hearted that he fainted at a hanging." It was a true story and worth the telling.

CHAPTER NINE

The Hanging of Dennis Dilda

THE FAINTING INCIDENT Pauline O'Neill recalled haunted Buckey long after it had been forgotten by most others. He was finally able to get it out of his mind by writing a short-story-confession about it five years later.

What was to bring Buckey O'Neill as a witness at the gallows started innocently enough in the summer of 1885 in the Williamson Valley, north of Prescott, when a Texan named Dennis W. Dilda drove a wagon into the valley, found an unencumbered plot of ground, and built a shack. Dilda had a wife, who some said was mentally incompetent, and two small ragamuffin children. He was himself a swarthy, sullen loner who ignored the friendly gestures of his new neighbors, seemed to be away from his house a great deal of the time, and had no apparent means of livelihood.

Not long after Dilda's arrival, chickens, turkeys, ducks, and occasionally calves began to be missed by valley residents; some even discovered groceries stolen from their homes. Since no such thievery had occurred before the newcomer's advent, Williamson Valley folk began to keep an eye on the brooding Dilda, and eventually this caution paid off. Dilda was spotted dragging a dead calf into the makeshift corral behind his shack. Yavapai County Sheriff William Mulvenon was notified and dispatched his deputy, Johnny Murphy, to investigate. The date was December 20.

Murphy didn't return and, after what seemed an inordinately long absence by his deputy, Sheriff Mulvenon set out for Wil-

liamson Valley himself. Dilda's wife and children were found
alone. Mrs. Dilda denied having seen Deputy Murphy and
claimed no knowledge of her husband's whereabouts. Mulvenon, not satisfied, rode to a nearby ranch to borrow a horse
and buckboard, deputizing two ranchmen to follow him back
to the Dilda house.

Mrs. Dilda was placed under arrest and the sheriff and his
deputies began a thorough search of the house and grounds.
Two freshly butchered calf heads were uncovered from a
shallow burial near the shack. Inside the single-room house, a
loose floorboard in a corner aroused the lawmen's suspicions.
Mulvenon pried the board free and found freshly turned dirt
scattered beneath it. A foot below the surface lay Deputy
Murphy's corpse, wrapped in an oat sack. Murphy had been
killed by a gunshot, apparently fired at long range.

As the stiffened body was placed on the buckboard, Mrs.
Dilda sobbed out her story to Mulvenon. Her husband had spied
the deputy riding toward the house and knew he was to be
arrested. He grabbed a rifle, poked it through a chink in the
shack's wall, and shot Murphy off his horse a hundred yards
distant. Dilda then dragged the body into the cabin and buried
it under the floor as his wife and terrified children looked on.
He then packed grub and a bedroll, jumped astride Murphy's
horse, and rode off.

Once Mrs. Dilda was locked up in Prescott, Sheriff Mulvenon set out with two Indian trackers to pick up Dilda's trail.
The posse found the trail leading northwestward toward Kingman, and Mohave County Sheriff Rosenberg was enlisted to
help in the search.

Dilda was captured without a struggle at Ash Fork, near
Kingman, and taken back to Prescott in irons to stand trial.

There appeared to be little evidence to support any verdict
but guilty, and frontier justice—particularly in murder cases
involving peace officers—was inexorably swift. Dilda was con-
victed and sentenced to hang on February 5, 1886—forty-seven
days after Murphy's killing.

Dennis Dilda, his wife Georgia, and children Fern and John (Sharlot Hall Museum).

Since the sheriff was obliged to arrange for any executions in his jurisdiction, Sheriff Mulvenon had the gallows built at Willow and West Gurley streets, where pine trees and snow-capped mountains formed a calendar-picture backdrop.

As the day of the public execution approached, the Prescott Grays—with Buckey O'Neill now their captain and commander —were assigned as guards at the scaffold.

On the morning of February 5, Dilda sprung a sizable leak in the county jail budget by eating gluttonously a last meal of breaded spring chicken, cream sauce, fried oysters, lamb chops, green peas, tenderloin steak with mushrooms, English pancakes with jelly, potatoes, bread, and coffee. This Henry VIII-style meal under his belt (some said it caused the hangman to recalculate the length of drop through the trap necessary to snap Dilda's neck), his jailers guided the prisoner to a waiting carriage.

Dilda, his hands tied behind his back, rode to the gallows sitting on his coffin in the back of the buckboard. At ten A.M. the condemned man saw the scaffold and the crowd that had gathered around it, kept at a proper distance by Captain O'Neill's Grays. Dilda was escorted up the steps to the hinged platform, blindfolded, and the noose placed about his neck and pulled snugly against his right ear. The Grays faced the gallows and snapped to attention; Buckey drew his sword and the militiamen presented arms.

At a signal the trap fell and Dilda dropped four feet to eternity. At the same instant, a bug-eyed Buckey O'Neill dropped to the ground in a dead faint.

Pauline recounted later, with doubtful logic, that her husband fainted "because he saw the wife and children of the murderer who were left behind to be the by-word of an indignant populace. The wife was ill, and the children were so small and innocent that their future lot seemed an awful one to him."

Jim McClintock always remembered how "disgusted" Buckey felt about the incident, but McClintock offered no explanation, either in his own or Buckey's words, for the fainting spell.

Ralph Keithley claimed that Buckey "was always quick to admit that he couldn't stand to see anyone killed when 'he didn't have a chance.' "

More likely, Buckey simply got sick. He had never seen a hanging before but somebody who *had*, probably a Whiskey Row cowman who had witnessed a lynching, must have given Captain O'Neill plenty of the grisly details.

Five years after the Prescott hanging, Buckey got it all off his chest in a story he wrote called "A Horse of the Hash-Knife Brand," which appeared in the *San Francisco Chronicle*. The tale concerned the cottonwood-tree lynching of a horse thief named Jack Stanley. Stanley obviously was Dennis Dilda, and the youngest of the Hashknife cowboys who helped string up the thief most certainly was Buckey O'Neill. Buckey ended his story this way:

A few heavings of the chest, two or three spasmodic bendings of the body at the knees and hips, a turning in of the arms. a blackening of the face, with turgid, protruding eyes and tongue. and then a relaxation of all the muscles of the body, and a form that a few minutes before had breathed and thought and feared. hangs straight and limp in the air, turning slowly around like a top that is about to cease spinning.

A few minutes afterward, three men leading a hash knife branded horse, saddled and bridled, look back from the top of the last ridge at the body still swaying as it will sway for days to come, until the vultures and the wind and the rope do their work. when the neck will give way and a mass of bones will lie scattered around the roots of the tree until the floods of another winter wash them out of sight. And then the three men ride back over the old San Carlos trail, while the youngest of the party shudders as he thinks how near he came to disgracing himself by fainting when the body first went into the air.

CHAPTER TEN

A Soft Berth for Judge O'Neill

ALTHOUGH THE DILDA execution marked an inauspicious beginning for 1886, the year proved to be a good one, typically frenetic, for Buckey O'Neill. Now firmly established in Prescott's social life, Buckey was prominent as newspaperman and as captain of the Grays. Nor was Pauline a stay-at-home; she became active in local literary and feminine clubs and had developed a keen interest in the woman's suffrage movement. The new O'Neill home, close to Whipple Barracks, had developed into a favorite socializing center. The Prescott Chatauqua Circle gathered there, and Buckey liked to show off by quoting from Byron in response to the roll call. Frequent visitors were the officers and wives from Whipple Barracks, permitting Buckey to question at length the progress of the Apache campaign. In March, Geronimo and twenty of his warriors, after surrendering to General George Crook, escaped. In April, General Nelson A. Miles replaced Crook and opened what became the final phase of the Apache campaign—leading to Geronimo's surrender on August 25. Buckey listened intently—and enviously—to reports of these developments. The Grays had never satisfied his yearning for a true taste of the military life.

Politics offered an even stronger beckoning and in the spring of the year he decided to toss his politically virginal white stetson into the ring as a candidate for Yavapai County probate judge. The post itself was exceedingly dull, consisting of work on wills and estates, and the race held little fascination for the average voter; but Buckey's candidacy seemed to promise a fresh breeze for the usually stagnant contest.

Buckey as captain of the Prescott Grays.

For one thing, Buckey had become an avowed Republican in a staunchly Democratic stronghold. The new governor, appointed by President Grover Cleveland, was Conrad Meyer Zulick, the seventh to hold the office. Taking office only the preceding November, Zulick had the distinction of being the first Democrat appointed governor of the Territory, and the prevailing political winds, naturally, were blowing for the Democrats—at least for a time.

Other interesting aspects of the race included the facts that the incumbent judge, rather lovingly called "Uncle Billy" Wilkerson, not only had held the post for a number of years but also was conveniently a Democrat to boot; Buckey was a Catholic (his mother's influence dictated this: John O'Neill had been a Protestant and prominent in the Masonic order), though certainly not fanatic about it—and Catholics, like Republicans, were minority folk. Furthermore, Buckey was a political novice, a maverick, and unpolitically, amusingly blunt about everything. He seemed to think "candidacy" had something to do with "candid."

In announcing for the office, Buckey gave the *Flagstaff Champion* this statement:

> . . . No "anxious public," the "solicitation of many friends," nor "the wishes of many prominent citizens" have made the slightest effort to "bluff" me into doing it. To be frank, it is not a case where the office is wearing itself out hunting for a man—not much! Here it is the man wearing himself out hunting the office, and rustling like Sheol to get it, for the simple reason that it is a soft berth, with a salary of $2,000 per annum attached. While in the way of special qualifications, I have no advantage over seventy-five percent of my fellow citizens in the County, yet I believe I am fully competant to discharge all the duties incident to the office in an efficient manner, if elected. If you coincide in this opinion, support me, if you see fit. If you do not, you will by no means jeopardize the safety of the universe by defeating me.

Aside from the startling candor of the statement, it is instructive to note that Buckey made no claim of being a lawyer—a qualification that could have been of great impact for any candidate seeking a judgeship.

One reaction in Yavapai County to Buckey's candidacy was the circulation of an anonymous slander sheet that proved to be the eye of the hurricane of his political debut. Every subsequent statement on Buckey's part was geared to the calumnies of the anonymous broadside; indeed, the entire campaign—on both sides—revolved around it. It read:

> The Probate Judge of this County . . . should be like Caesar's wife —above suspicion.
> The question is: Does Mr. O'Neill fill this bill? W. O. O'Neill is well educated, wields a ready pen, and, were he possessed of those moral traits which adorn and elevate true manhood, would be a citizen we would all delight to honor.
> Unfortunately he is not so constituted. W. O. O'Neill is known far and wide as "Buckey" O'Neill, because of his fondness for faro, and the dash and recklessness with which, when in funds, he piles the red and white chips upon his favorite card.

He is also a drunkard. Though young in years, his bleared eye and flushed face give evidence that the nights of dissipation—the days of continuous drunks—are slowly but surely undermining a naturally strong and vigorous constitution.

Then, throwing Buckey's *Champion* statement back in his face, the anonymous writer continued:

He prides himself upon being a spoilsman—openly declares that no higher principle governs his political actions than the spoils of office. Confessedly a mountebank among men, he is a libertine among women; glorying in his vices, he assails all that is reputable in manhood, or chaste and virtuous in womanhood.

To confirm what is herein said as to his peculiar views of obligations a public officer owes to the people, and the qualifications necessary to secure it in Arizona, read his announcement of his candidature for the office of Probate Judge.

In a last burst of frontier-style libel, the circular addressed a few choice slanders at the state of the O'Neill marriage:

It is claimed by his friends that "Buckey" has reformed since his marriage. That such a statement is untrue is well authenticated. His neighbors know that in the small hours of the morning he has been taken home to his waiting and expectant bride in a state of beastly intoxication, introducing into his home that brutality which adheres to every animated specimen of total depravity.

The circular was signed "Committee of Stockmen" as if to appeal to those who might still entertain the notion that the *Hoof and Horn* editor had any respectability among the cattle fraternity.

Buckey's response to the leaflet was published in the *Prescott Journal-Miner* which already had announced its support of the O'Neill campaign:

It is an act worthy of the murderous instincts of an assassin who lacks the nerve to strike the fatal blow. An act only worthy of a man who will stab in the dark, or beat the brains out of an unsuspecting fellow-being from behind. . . . If there be truth in the circular, I challenge its author to face me and give me an opportunity in the broad light of day, and in the open sight of the brave men and women with whom I have lived and toiled nearly ten years, to meet it. . . .

The *Journal-Miner* commented that the "Committee of Stockmen" leaflet would "act as a boomerang upon its authors, and elect W. O. O'Neill Probate Judge."

The backlash against the stockmen's screed received an official sanction when Morris Goldwater (great uncle of Arizona's U.S. Senator Barry Goldwater), secretary of the County Democratic Central Committee, published a "card" addressed to Buckey in the Prescott papers, which read:

On behalf of the Democracy of Yavapai County and in the name of the Democratic Central Committee of such County, I desire to disclaim and repudiate any connection of our party with the slanderous and cowardly attack which has been made from some anonymous source on you as being not only undemocratic, but so vile and unprincipled as to merit the just censure and condemnation of all fair minded men.

And a group signing itself "Young Democracy" published its view that the stockmen's canard would propel O'Neill to victory:

. . . despite the sneers of lisping dudes and the serpent tongues of brutal bigots, he will be elected by a large majority in the mountains and valleys. His friends are legion. not the least of whom are the young democracy who will show their independence of cliques by voting for the brilliant young editor.

Throughout the campaign, while Buckey stumped for votes in the back reaches of enormous Yavapai County, the *Journal-Miner* kept up a drumfire of editorial comment on the O'Neill campaign. On October 26 the paper carried the notice: "The dirty attacks upon W. O. O'Neill are making him more popular every day." And on November 3, writing on Buckey's Democratic opponent—the man heavily endorsed in saccharine terms by the *Prescott Courier*—the *Journal-Miner* noted: " 'Uncle Billy' Wilkerson says he knew nothing about the abusive circular against W. O. O'Neill. Maybe he didn't. We happen to know that he was notified very quickly about it and his disclaimer comes at a very late date."

When the votes were tallied in mid-November, Buckey got

the scare of his political life. He had run hard, scaling steep mountainsides to drop in on obscure mining camps, talking it up in every knot of people he could find willing to listen. In the meantime, "Uncle Billy" lay back, apparently trusting his incumbency and the support of the *Courier*, plus his Democratic Party affiliation, to shoo him in. On the night of the ballot count it was rumored that Uncle Billy stayed home eating a great oyster dinner in celebration of his impending reelection. If so, about midway through he lost his appetite.

Although Buckey had a terrific scare, when the paper was sorted and tallied he had squeaked in—*eight votes* ahead of Wilkerson, the smallest spread of any candidate on the ballot, Republican or Democrat.

Eight votes or eight hundred, he was now Judge Buckey O'Neill.

CHAPTER ELEVEN

Buckey of All Trades

 CAPTAIN O'NEILL and the Grays gathered on New Year's Day, 1887, as honor guard for Governor Zulick, who drove a golden spike to mark the arrival of the long-awaited Prescott and Arizona Central Railroad at Prescott Junction. Joining in the festivities were two local volunteer fire companies, a detachment of soldiers from Fort Whipple, and a crowd of hundreds on horseback, in carriages, and afoot. Two locomotives—*Governor Frederick H. Tritle* and *Pueblo*—pulled in amid the roar of Fort Whipple cannon, the scream of steam whistles, and the cheers of onlookers.

Buckey, unable to conceal his nervousness, paced anxiously while he awaited the end of the long and tedious ceremony. Pauline, ill with her pregnancy, had shown some signs of early labor and Buckey worried that a crisis might develop while he fulfilled his duty with the militia several miles from home.

On January 4 Pauline delivered a son, delicately premature but alive and squalling nonetheless. Buckey's political ally and promoter, the *Journal-Miner*, got the honor of announcing the event:

Judge W. O. O'Neill had a smile on his countenance this morning which spread clear across the street, and a step so elastic that he could almost walk on air. . . . Later in the day, a package containing a half dozen bottles of claret arrived accompanied by the following explanation of the situation: "Compliments of 'Buckey' O'Neill, Jr."

Tragically, the smile and springy step had disappeared when, exactly two weeks later, the *Miner* sadly reported, "The infant child of Mr. and Mrs. W. O. O'Neill is very sick and not expected to live."

"Buckey, Jr.," died a few days later, victim of the virulent infections that doomed so many premature infants in a day of still-primitive frontier medicine.

The baby's death naturally was a crushing blow to the O'Neills, but Buckey had new duties to perform. He flung himself into his work with a vengeance. He found the probate court suffocating in a backlog of paperwork, particularly an enormous pile of unsettled estate reports that had choked the docket book for years. To his amazement, he discovered that much of the cost of settling these delinquent accountings fell directly and legally on the probate judge's shoulders. His first official act, therefore, was to rid the court of this odious and ridiculous ruling by writing a sharp letter to the Yavapai County Board of Supervisors asking to be relieved of all expenses accruing to the settlement of estates. The supervisors agreed and provided the new judge with a small allotment to settle pending cases and bring delinquent ones to his court.

Buckey took the board's response as a mandate to clean up the probate docket. He ran advertising in Prescott's newspapers notifying estate administrators to settle up with the county, and armed the sheriff with attachments on properties subject to probate. Response to these measures made the probate court busy once again, and even newsworthy, though many estate attorneys and other principals in pending or long-delayed cases were found either to have died or "Left the Territory." Still, as one paper reported, "Judge O'Neill has done more to get the affairs of the probate court in order than any of his predecessors."

Of much greater interest to Judge O'Neill than the bone-dry business of wills, codicils, beneficiaries, and contestors, was his ex officio status as county superintendent of schools—heretofore little more than a nominal and gratuitous duty. Buckey clearly recalled that when Governor Zulick had addressed the Fourteenth Territorial Legislature in March, he could not resist bragging that 130 school districts and 13 new school houses had been built the previous year. To Buckey that was all very nice but hardly the point. He knew that the governor knew that scarcely one-third of the Territory's school-age children actually were attending school. It appeared to the new Yavapai County school superintendent that his ex officio position might enable him to do something about that situation.

As his initial move, Buckey fired off a typically cocksure letter to the territorial superintendent of schools, C. M. Strauss. Columns of figures attached showed that only about three school-age youngsters out of every ten in Arizona actually were receiving formal schooling. The letter began with a reasonable observation: Part of the fault lay in the fact that schools in the Territory were open only six months of the year, "although the taxpayers of Arizona contribute more in proportion to their taxable property than do the taxpayers of any other Territory" toward school construction, salaries, and the like. Buckey's letter ended, however, with a withering blast at the territorial superintendent himself—Buckey's boss in school affairs—which equated the failure of the schools with "the number of leeches who have attached themselves to the school system for appropriating to their own use the money which should go to educating the young."

Leading into his angry and precipitate censure of Strauss' office, Buckey compared the number of Arizona school officials drawing pay from the territorial treasury to "the Haytien army," where, he said, "the number of officers is limited by the number of uniforms." Then he proceeded to earn himself a certain enemy:

Take as an example the office of Territorial Superintendent, created to please a Prescott pedagogue. Originally a sinecure, it has never ceased to be one. The only change in it has been in the salary, which has been increased until today the incumbent draws yearly from the treasury of the Territory $3,000 as traveling expenses etc. etc. In return for this sum the Territory receives nothing, while the Superintendent spends his time sojourning wherever pleasure may call him. From the outset the office has been a barnacle, a parasite, a fungus, and will continue to be while it lasts.

Understandably, Superintendent Strauss became more than a little exercised over this cup of gall. He soon countered Buckey's dynamite charge with a firecracker of his own, accusing the upstart probate judge with "misapportioning" Yavapai County School funds. Later, opposing political forces would translate this to "mis-*appropriating*" school funds, a far graver offense, and would hit candidate O'Neill over the head with it.

But, by then, candidate O'Neill would be fighting a war on another front too: an old matter involving Judge Dan Pinney of Lockport, Illinois.

Whatever toes Buckey tromped on, his furious assault on Arizona's scandalous school attendence record paid dividends. It took twelve years to pay them, but Buckey received credit for helping prompt the Legislature in 1899 to pass Arizona's first compulsory school-attendance law.

Pauline was recovering both medically and emotionally from the birth and death of Buckey, Jr., and the O'Neill household was returning to normal. Buckey, who could barely endure the sadness that followed their great loss, kept each hour filled— work in court, writing at home, thinking in both places, and, of course, keeping up with the happenings on Whiskey Row.

One of these latter events took place in April when Buckey was elected second assistant foreman of the "Toughs," Hose Company Number One of Prescott's volunteer fire department. The Toughs comprised a group of about 25 volunteers, largely drawn from Whiskey Row establishments—saloon owners, gamblers and miners. Their equipment, conveniently stabled in a wooden building about midway up the Row, consisted of a 2-wheel, hand-drawn horse cart, and about 600 feet of 2½-inch canvas hose with a polished brass nozzle.

Buckey's Toughs were among four volunteer companies of the PVFD; the others being the Dudes Hose Company Number Two (called the "Dudes"); the O.K. Hose Company Number

Three—the "OK's"; and the Mechanics Hook and Ladder Company Number One—called not the "Mechanics" but the "Hooks."

Aside from the noble aspects of being a volunteer fireman—and Prescott had plenty of need for such services—other perquisites included the right to wear the special uniform of the day: fire-engine red shirts, snappy caps, and patent-leather belts. Other necessities were provided from the volunteers' own wardrobe. Moreover, there was the accessory right to take part in the volunteers' ongoing "social activities."

Few of the PVFD's periodic meetings were ever dry and the meetings of Buckey's "Toughs" were *never* dry. Someone always brought a keg (or as it was called, a "kag") of beer, bung, and starter, and meetings often were devoted solely to "social activity" planning. Such sessions usually consisted of dances and, more exciting, contests to see which hose company could race its cart 200 yards down the Row, lay 250 feet of hose, connect it to a fire plug, attach nozzle, and begin spraying water. The 12-man teams would train up to 2 months for these contests. Heavy wagering on the side spurred all to their best efforts.

Unfortunately for Buckey, the Toughs seldom made better than second place, the Dudes being perennial winners (some said because they trained less on beer and more on running). But the Toughs played second to none in the aftermath ritual of soaking up Whiskey Row refreshments.

For the Toughs, Dudes, OK's and Hooks, all was not beer bust and cart race. Whiskey Row itself, where the volunteers kept their equipment, seemed a perpetual tinderbox. On January 5, 1883, a saloon fire resulted in ninety thousand dollars damages on the Row. On July 14, 1890, a fire starting in a miner's shanty on the Row would nearly wipe out the town, burning the bank, hotels, stores, newspaper plants, and scores of dwellings to the ground. The very year Buckey joined the force, on November 19, a boiler in a Prescott sawmill exploded, killing six workmen and threatening to spread down the Row and into town before being contained.

Buckey's eight years in the Territory had convinced him that Arizona possessed untapped agricultural possibilities if water sources could be found, an even brighter future as a health resort and retirement spa. Both ideas, his friends liked to say in later years, were visionary and far ahead of their time.

At about the time he purchased the equipment to begin publishing *Hoof and Horn*, Buckey had invested one thousand dollars in a few parcels of land in the Phoenix area, possibly through the advice of his friend Jim McClintock. As a result, and particularly with increased murmurings over the possibility of moving the territorial capital to Phoenix, Buckey watched closely the economic growth of his first Arizona city of residence. With a group of friends, he also invested in the Buckeye Irrigation Canal serving the Salt River valley, thirty miles west of Phoenix, and running along the Salt River southwest of Phoenix between Liberty and Coldwater.

This region became a major farming locale in early Arizona because of the availability of water. Jack Swilling, the Confederate deserter and outlaw, had organized an irrigation company in the area in the 1860's and ten years later a population of more than three hundred had been attracted to the place then called "Pumpkinville," later to be given the more dignified name of Phoenix.

The Buckeye Canal instilled in Buckey O'Neill a deep interest in irrigation possibilities for the entire Territory. To a Fort Whipple acquaintance, W. A. Glassford, he often launched into lengthy monologues on the "cause" of irrigation. Glassford later wrote, " . . . he evolved the idea of getting the government to take up the reclamation of arid regions. He used to argue that Congress appropriated for the rivers, harbors, and waterways of the East, to bring commerce to agriculture so why not appropriate to promote agriculture? He said that as agriculture was the basis of commerce, even of civilization, why not do something for agriculture in the arid West?"

As a result of his forward-looking attitude toward the canal project, irrigation and reclamation possibilities, and other dreams of great progress for the stepchild Territory, Judge O'Neill became a one-man chamber of commerce for the idea of Arizona as a health and retirement center. In the spring of 1887, Buckey turned out a 130-page book (on the back cover of which he listed himself as "William O. O'Neill, Real Estate Agent") on "Resources of Northern Arizona," and a companion tract on "Central Arizona for Homes, for Health." The *Prescott Journal-Miner* thought highly of both efforts and quoted extensively from them. In the latter pamphlet, Buckey wrote:

What Italy might be from a climatic standpoint, if freed from its miasmatic poisons, Central Arizona is. On no other portion of the globe, unless it be the high plateau of the Himalayas or Andes, can such a flawless climate be found.

. . . Arizona is one of the healthiest regions of the world, and the figures of the United States Census for 1880 fully attest to this. Let the invalid seeking restoration to health before deciding where he shall go to find it, consider this fact well.

Elsewhere in his promotional tract, he said ecstatically:

If pure air there be, it is here. . . . The step grows elastic and one feels as though he had drunk of the fabulous fountain of eternal youth. And so it is throughout the years. The feeling of listless lassitude, which elsewhere makes life a burden, is never felt here.

Buckey wrote these effusions at night, at home. He especially liked to write while Pauline played the piano. He began to think in terms of fiction, too, and experimented with short stories with Western settings, sending a few of them to San Francisco newspapers. To his amazement, the *Examiner*—William Randolph Hearst's newly-acquired paper—offered space rates for them and asked for more.

Despite these time-consuming endeavors, Buckey found time occasionally to prop his feet on his court office desk, roll a fag, and chat with drop-in friends. M. B. Haziltine, later president of the Bank of Arizona, recalled one such conversation, observing that Buckey's salutation was always the same: "Well, Mose, what's new?" Haziltine said his usual response was that he knew nothing new and that this generally served to stoke

Buckey's always-smoldering conversational fire. On this particular occasion, Buckey said: "You know what I would like to
do, Mose? I would like to take fifty thousand dollars and invest
it at four percent and then go back to Washington and just
simply live at the Library of Congress and study about social-
ism."

"You know, Buckey," Haziltine responded, "fifty thousand
dollars at four percent would only bring you two thousand dollars a year and you would only get one thousand of *that*."

"Why is that?" said Buckey, his roll-your-own bouncing on
his lip.

"Well, being a socialist you would have to give me half of it."

Buckey's fingers came to his mouth in a "V" and removed the
butt. With a grin he answered, "Mose, I only divide what I
haven't got."

CHAPTER TWELVE

The Conquistador of Yavapai County

THE FIFTEENTH LEGISLATURE, convening in January, 1888, proved to be the last to meet in Buckey's town of Prescott. The move to transfer the territorial capital to Phoenix had been afoot for some time and, although Governor Zulick had become a lame duck with Benjamin Harrison's defeat of President Cleveland, he signed the final paper on January 26. Legislative Act Number One of the Fifteenth Legislature decreed, "On and after the Fourth Day of February, in the year of our Lord Eighteen Hundred and Eighty-Nine, the permanent seat of Government and Capital of this Territory shall be, and the same is, hereby located and established at the City of Phoenix, in the County of Maricopa."

Buckey was as politically ambitious as any man in the Territory. Yet if he gave a thought to packing up and moving Pauline and the household to Phoenix to remain close to territorial politics, there is no record of it. In fact, his eye already had trained on the most powerful office in his home county of Yavapai—that of sheriff.

Much like his race for the probate judgeship, which revolved almost solely around the stockmen screed, Buckey's political stetson, now decidedly soiled from its previous venture into the ring, scarcely had hit the ground when the issues were drawn. "The issues" was territorial newspaper language for whatever assortment of scandal, innuendo, and outright calumny could be heaped on the man opposing the paper's favorite. Actually there was only one issue, and Buckey's detractors were determined to make the most of it.

As his first step toward the sheriff's office, Buckey had to seek the nomination of his party. As it fortuitously worked out, the party proved to be seeking him. When the Yavapai County Republican caucus met in the summer of 1888, Buckey won his nomination by acclamation, and no one raised an eyebrow when the Democrats renominated Joseph R. Walker, the incumbent sheriff, now finishing his second term.

The opening dose of campaign grapeshot was fired by Buckey's prime nemesis in the judgeship race, the *Prescott Courier*, which began by referring to the Republican caucus that had nominated Judge O'Neill as "the Ring."

The Ring candidate, W. O. O'Neill, had no opposition in the ratification meeting. He is now Probate Judge of this county; has lived mostly off taxes ever since he came to Prescott; tried to set stockman against miner; stultified himself in many ways and cannot be elected by the Ring.
. . . He cannot defeat old Joe Walker, prospector, miner, Indian fighter, stockraiser, and good man generally.

A week later the *Courier* rounded out its original mouthful by introducing in quick succession, the other "issues" of Buckey's birthright and religion:

It is said that every Irish Catholic in the county will vote for O'Neill. We have a better opinion of Catholics in the county than to believe that they can be driven to the polls like so many sheep, to vote for a man whose pants' knees scarcely ever touch the church floor.

For all that, the greatest of the campaign "issues" had yet to be introduced. A few more weeks were to pass before it cropped up to stay.

In the meantime, Buckey set out to stump the county. Unlike running for probate judge, a post few people could define and fewer still cared to, the sheriff's race drew everyone's interest. "Law and order," a catch-phrase in the 1880's as much as today, described a real issue.

The remotest mining claims thus received a visit from Judge O'Neill, and it became clear that he already had earned a certain measure of affection among these hard-drinking, hard-working men. Men who never had voted before were impressed with his sense of urgency about the race. They also hankered to hear his recital of experience under the fine Phoenix marshal Enrique (Henry) Garfias, his status as captain of the Grays, his service as volunteer fireman, and his hard work and accomplishments as probate judge and school superintendent. On the latter point, his "barnacle" letter to the territorial superintendent, Strauss, had been well publicized and had resulted in an almost universal mining-camp guffaw and collective clap on the back for its author. But mostly, Buckey impressed men by his candor and his easy and sincere enjoyment of hard-scrabbling men. He could take a drink, twirl a brown-paper "nail," and trade a currently ripe story with the best of them. It was grass-roots politics among the mine tailings.

Buckey dwelt on no particular issue in the campaign; his was an appeal based mostly on "let-me-have-a-go-at-it." But he did delight in saying that if elected he had a plan to right a serious injustice to the taxpayer. The sheriff's office, like that of probate judge, carried with it an additional ex officio responsibility. The county's chief law enforcement officer also was its tax assessor-collector, and Buckey declared he would assess the railroad, for the first time, the full value of its land holdings.

On the face of it, this idea does not appear startling, but in Arizona Territory in the 1880's, it signified raw naivete and bald unsophistication at best and, at worst, certain political suicide. Political and economic power coursed out along the tentacles of the railroad to such an extent that railroads and power were virtually synonymous. By simply flowing a certain direction, these tentacles could nourish a city, a state, or a territory, and make it thrive; by delay or altering course, they could cause these same cities, states, and territories to wither or remain in the backwater, starved of progress. The railroads, extending back to the power source, demanded certain concessions—tax adjustments, rights-of-way, and land grants—and got them. To tinker with this system was, at the very least, to court

danger, and no seasoned politician dared do so in Arizona in
the 1880's.

By the end of September the sheriff's campaign began to
warm. Sheriff Walker, like Buckey's earlier opponent, Uncle
Billy Wilkerson, seemed to be lying back, putting considerable
faith in the *Courier* to carry his message of incumbency, performance, record as soldier and lawman, fearlessness, friend of
all. The *Courier*, dutifully doing its work for Walker, on September 29 aimed its secret weapon at Buckey: "Will the
Journal-Miner inform the taxpayers," the *Courier* rhetorically
asked of Buckey's ally, "what benefit they received from the
$500 Judge O'Neill secured from them by special act of the
13th Legislature?"

Buckey had known it would come. Back in March, in a news
item about Judge O'Neill, someone had quoted the irrepressible
Judge D. H. Pinney of Lockport, Illinois, as saying "I had no
court reporter from July, 1882 to January 1, 1883," and Pinney
had repeated his contention that the five-hundred-dollar payment to Buckey by special act of the "Thieving Thirteenth"
was "a first-class steal." Pinney also reminded his interviewer
that he had expressed his indignation to Governor Tritle by
telegram as soon as he had learned of it.

The *Courier's* sanctimony over the five hundred dollars sur-
passed that of Judge Pinney. It loaded the same cannoball over
and over, pulling the lanyard almost daily to repeat the charge
that Buckey had "taken" five hundred dollars for two days'
court reporting, fondly repeating the Pinney quote, and re-
minding all and sundry that Pinney was a Republican himself
and therefore had no political axe to grind.

Buckey was confronted with the question everywhere he
went, so well had the *Courier* engraved it on the public mind,
but his tactic was to be blithe about it. To one reporter he said,
"Judge Pinney had just come to the Territory from Illinois and
was not acquainted with Arizona prices." Another of Buckey's
responses particularly appalled the *Courier*, which had long

since passed the point of recognizing humor in so grave an issue as the "first-class steal." Buckey was reported as saying in answer to the five-hundred-dollar question: "Hell, I would have taken *fifteen hundred!*"

He couldn't have planned a better counterattack.

Close now to election day, the *Courier* stepped up its assault, committing one of the campaign's most memorable typographical faux pas: "Every citizen who loves fair play," announced the paper on October 13, "will endeavor to keep the ballot boxes from being stuffed with fraudulent voters [*sic*] . . . he [O'Neill] is a chronic office-seeker and office-holder."

Buckey thus was indicted for his one year on the probate court bench as a "chronic office-holder," whatever that was.

Belatedly, the *Courier* also charged Judge O'Neill with "being accused of" misappropriating monies from his school superintendent coffers and diverting them to his own use. That Buckey had no control over or access to such funds, and that the original accusation by territorial Superintendent Strauss had to do with mis*apportioning* funds, was duly explained, and this eleventh hour "issue" died on the vine.

On election day, November 7, 1888, Whiskey Row closed down and Buckey, detained on a last-minute speech-making stint in Flagstaff, managed to return on the new railroad line just hours after the official vote tally came in. He stepped off the Prescott and Central to meet Pauline to the blare of the Ninth Infantry Band and a crowd of friends and onlookers. There could be little doubt as to the decision of the electorate.

The next day the *Courier* grimly reported the election results, throwing in an outsized bunch of sour grapes to season its tight-lipped account:

. . . it was charged that vote purchasing was much indulged in. Judge O'Neill, sheriff-elect, was met at the depot last evening on his return from Flagstaff, by a great many of his admirers, in carriage and on foot. They had the Ninth Infantry band, torches, etc. The procession marched through the principal streets and cheered as it went.

The *Courier* did not mention, of course, the rampant rumors that the Atlantic and Pacific Railroad had rushed in section hands from a radius of a hundred miles to stuff the ballot box against the man who talked about adjusting their taxes.

The returns, unlike the squeak-in as probate judge, showed Buckey winning in all districts in the county except Kirkland Valley, where he and Walker took eleven votes each, and Saguara, where he lost to Walker, ten to six.

Buckey's old newspaper, the *Phoenix Herald*, reported the Prescott returns and, noting that Judge O'Neill had pulled the second of two upsets in a row, called the sheriff-elect "the Conquistador of Yavapai County." It had a nice ring to it.

CHAPTER THIRTEEN

Long Ride from Diablo Canyon

BEFORE TAKING over his new office, Buckey had one matter to clear up in his old one. Territorial Superintendent of Schools Strauss, in his countercharge to Judge O'Neill's hip-shot "barnacle-parasite-fungus" letter, had mentioned the word "misapportionment." The word had been freely translated by Buckey's opponents to "misappropriation," and the new sheriff realized it would be unwise to leave it hanging over his head, in either form, as he tried to epitomize county law and order. Thus, when a grand jury examining team came to look over the books of the probate court, Buckey was relieved of the burden of proving his innocence. The examiners scoured dockets, files, reports, and ledgers and wrote to their superiors:

It is with pleasure your committee can report that Judge O'Neill has made an efficient and trustworthy officer; having as far as we can learn transacted the affairs of his office to the satisfaction of the county. Judge O'Neill is to be especially commended for the zeal and impartiality he has manifested in the settlement of a large number of estates during his official tenure.

As to Superintendent Strauss' charge of "misapportionment," the grand jury reported to District Judge James Wright that "the said charges simply involve a construction of the school law," and it was unceremoniously dropped at that.

Soon after New Year's Day, 1889, Buckey received from outgoing Sheriff Walker the Hassayampa gold badge of the Yavapai County Sheriff's Department and took over Walker's quarters. Aside from some routine arrests—the first a common thief on January 15—Buckey had time to twist and light a cigarette, read the wanted posters, and study the state of law enforcement in his own county and around it. Over in the Tonto Bàsin, just northeast of Phoenix, the chief territorial law problem raged on, writing a scorching chapter in Arizona history. The Graham-Tewksbury Feud (or Pleasant Valley War, as some, loving the irony of the name, were calling it) had to do with resolving the issue of sheep in cattle country by the expediencies of murder and terrorism. According to one estimate, the war cost the lives of twenty-nine men before it ended in August, 1892.

Yavapai County was enjoying a period of relative calm though, and Buckey devoted his first couple of months in office to helping restore civic pride in the town, a commodity that had slipped noticeably with the removal of the territorial capital to Phoenix. Finding that he could put county prisoners to work on beautification projects, he obtained from the city fathers their ready agreement and a small appropriation to buy saplings. He had elm, box elder, and birch trees planted around the town plaza, and the area was policed up, swept, and watered daily.

With all that tranquility, hell simply had to break loose. Buckey had a peculiar knack of being in the right place at the wrong time—or perhaps the right time depending on how you look at it. Who else could have been court reporter five years earlier when Patrick McAteer's mind snapped, driving him to his bloody rampage? Who else could have joined the Prescott Volunteer Fire Department just before Whiskey Row nearly burned down? Who else could have been newly named captain of the Prescott Grays in time to watch the hanging of Dennis Dilda? Who else could have been three months in office as sheriff when the Diablo Canyon train robbery was pulled off?

The fact that Buckey was fresh and untried, the polish yet to be worn off his new gold badge, only added to the luster of the dime-novel, Ned Buntline-like scenario that unfolded in the spring of 1889. The incident, more than any other in his career prior to 1898, would afford him a secure place in the Valhalla of Arizona heroes.

On March 19, Will C. Barnes and William Broadbent rode into Winslow trailing four men who had robbed the Barnes ranch at the mouth of Box Canyon on the Chevellons fork of the Little Colorado River, between Holbrook and Winslow. Barnes, a Medal of Honor hero and veteran of Southwestern Indian wars, knew little about the bandits except that one of them was wearing a Mexican sombrero and carried a white-handled six-shooter.

The next day, at Diablo Canyon, twenty-four miles west of Winslow, the four robbers struck again. The Atlantic and Pacific Eastbound Number Two, a passenger train, had stopped at the canyon to replenish its woodbox at about eleven o'clock in the evening. As the train ground to a halt, four men boarded her. Holding the crew at gunpoint, they forced open the express safe, taking some seven thousand dollars in cash, and miscellaneous jewelry, including watches and a set of diamond earrings.

The four bandits were William Sterin, John Halford, Daniel Harvick, and J. J. Smith, all cowhands with the Hashknife outfit of the Aztec Land and Cattle Company, headquartered opposite the Mormon village of Saint Joseph, on the Little Colorado. Having left the ranch singly over a period of a week before robbing the Barnes ranch, they had gathered near Box Canyon to lay further plans.

About five miles south of the Diablo Canyon station, the four men divided the loot into even piles. Smith got the diamond earrings and, after removing them from their settings, put the loose stones into his pocket. He forgot about them and later scraped the stones out of his pocket and put them with tobacco crumbs into his pipe. When he knocked the ashes out on the heel of his boot, the diamonds were lost.

After splitting the express-box take, the robbers crossed the railroad tracks ten miles west of Winslow and rode to the northwest, heading for Lee's Ferry on the Big Colorado, camping above the ferry on the rim of Glen Canyon until nightfall.

Buckey and his deputy, James L. Black, were at Flagstaff on business when the Diablo Canyon robbery took place. Receiving word of it on the afternoon of March 21, they left for the scene early next morning. Rewards posted totaled four thousand dollars, which the *Prescott Journal-Miner* predicted optimistically "will no doubt be promptly paid to the officers who have so persistently followed the trail of the robbers."

Buckey and Jim Black, joined by Special Deputy Ed St. Clair of Flagstaff and Carl Holton, special detective for the A. and P., followed the still-warm trail north into the heart of the Painted Desert. There, on a Navajo Indian reservation, Buckey and his men met up with Will Barnes and his trackers. A young Navajo

The Diablo Canyon Posse: Left to right, Carl Holton, Jim Black, Buckey, and Ed St. Clair (Sharlot Hall Museum).

boy was sent to the railhead at Winslow with a message telling
the direction the bandits had taken and urging that settlements
in southern Utah be alerted to watch for the fugitives.

Sheriff O'Neill's posse reached the crossing at Lee's Ferry[5]
toward the end of the month to learn that the fugitives had
crossed two days before. Encamped in a southern Utah settlement, Buckey and his riders learned that the robbers had headed
in the direction of Wah Weep Canyon, a Mormon settlement
near Cannonville. On arriving at Wah Weep, however, they
again picked up the trail, heading south, the four outlaws apparently hoping to confuse their pursuers by doubling back
toward the ferry.

Not far out of Wah Weep Canyon, Buckey came across the
carcass of a slaughtered steer and, nearby, a deserted camp,
with ashes still warm and fresh horse and boot tracks in ample
evidence. Following the tracks and turning a sharp corner in
the canyon, Buckey caught a glimpse of one fleeing man, apparently a lookout, and got off a quick shot that brought down
the rider's mount. Soon a hail of exchanged pistol shots criss-
crossed the pine and juniper trees in the canyon's mouth. A
stray shot struck Buckey's horse squarely in the head, dropping
the animal instantly and pinning the sheriff momentarily
beneath it.

The four bandits' horses, scampering off into the hills at the
reverberating gunfire, left the fugitives afoot and Buckey, freed
from beneath his dead horse by one of his possemen, soon had
Halford and Sterin in irons. Smith and Harvick were captured
a short time later. A thorough search of the men and their recaptured horses turned up a large amount of currency in saddlebags, as well as several gold coins and a gold watch.

The pursuit had taken nearly three weeks, covering a trail
some six hundred miles long. And it wasn't over yet.

Sheriff O'Neill decided to remove his prisoners to Salt Lake
City, three hundred miles due north, and return them thence to

[5] The ferry had been established by John D. Lee, the only Mormon executed for
his part in the Mountain Meadows Massacre of 1857.

Prescott by rail. It would be a roundabout journey over three rail lines which, when traced on a map, appears as a lopsided pentagon with the Four Corners area near the center.

At Panguitch, Utah, a local blacksmith hammered leg irons onto the prisoners. The group then continued up the Sevier River by wagon to Marysvale, the first railhead, the four hapless prisoners chained together. Buckey, his posse, and the captives, on the evening of April 10, reached Salt Lake City, where the proper papers were secured. Then the trail-weary party continued by rail to Denver, there to commence the long journey south by the Santa Fe line.

In Prescott, meantime, the new governor had issued a congratulatory telegram to the newspapers:

W. O. O'Neill, Prescott, Arizona: The undersigned most heartily congratulate you on your successful capture of the train robbers after so persistent and dangerous a trip. The people of Arizona and the country in general are proud of your achievement and are deeply grateful. [Signed] Louis A. Wolfley, Governor.

The long Santa Fe train now rolled through the westward slope of Raton Pass. Prisoner J. J. Smith, testing his leg irons— a configuration of chain and shackle called an "Oregon Boot"— learned that he could pull his boot off and slip the ring over one ankle. He did so at a propitious nighttime moment and escaped near the town of Raton.

When Smith's escape was discovered not long afterward, Buckey was awakened and informed of it. Later, one of the prisoners wrote, "His language to the thoroughly awakened deputies was fluent and to the point . . . he seized the bell cord and stopped the train." After six hours of searching, Buckey flagged a westbound woodburner and rode back to Raton to join his party—minus J. J. Smith.

On April 15, Buckey's guards marched the three remaining prisoners into the Yavapai County Jail at Prescott. In their preliminary hearing, the captives faced only two witnesses. These were E. G. Knickerbocker, the express manager whose safe had been robbed at Diablo Canyon, and Deputy Jim Black who, with Buckey, had followed the trail of the four men from the platform of the Diablo Station until their capture. The judge ordered the robbers held over for appearance before a grand jury but, prior to their trial, the three culprits agreed to plead guilty with the understanding that each would be sentenced to twenty-five years in the Yuma Territorial Prison.

Before they were removed to Yuma, J. J. Smith—who had escaped all the way to Vernon, Texas, near the Red River-Oklahoma border—was recaptured and returned to Prescott. An extra five years was tacked onto his sentence after he, too, had pleaded guilty.

John Halford and Daniel Harvick went to the Yuma "Hellhole" on July 22, 1889, William Sterin on July 28, each to serve twenty-five years. J. J. Smith reached the prison on November 24 facing a thirty-year sentence.

Buckey, meantime, totaled up expenses and came up with a figure of a little more than $8,000 for the 3-week, 4-state, 600-mile trek. The Prescott Board of Supervisors agreed to pay $5,800 of the amount but balked at the remainder. Their expense sheet and Buckey's didn't jibe; perhaps the memory of Buckey's $500-payment for 2 days' court reporting stuck in their minds. The argument advanced by the supervisors, however, concerned the sheriff's exceeding his jurisdiction; the pursuit outside the Territory, while laudable for its successful conclusion, hardly fell within the scope of territorial reimbursement.

Buckey, never one to avoid jumping headlong into the breach when it came to money matters, determined to sue for the difference. On Christmas Eve, 1889, the judge of the district court in Prescott not only agreed with Buckey's accounting on the Diablo Canyon case, but delivered a grandiloquent, Walter Scott-like summation of the matter. It began:

Never did Roderic Dhu, winding his hunter's horn along the echoing shores of Loch Katrine, or Robin Hood in his largest sphere of freebooting, summon clans to more deadly intent than did the leader, Smith, with his gang of desperate highwaymen, upon fell purpose go.

One can almost see the judge counting the feet and measuring the meter as he chisled a decision he was sure not only would stand up under any appeal, but also might stand as a sort of monument to the arid literature of law. He continued:

In an almost incredibly short time . . . Yavapai County's young sheriff with his rough riders, is in the saddle; and now commences that pursuit which, as detailed by the evidence in this case, has scarcely a parallel for daring and pertinacity in this or any other country. Across vast sandy plains, up and over rugged mesas and mountains, through cañons and mountain gorges . . . the pursuit is waged; till at last the robbers are overtaken—a fight ensues . . . and the robbers are all captured. But it is over the Utah line; and it is contended for this reason, forsooth, the Sheriff can get nothing for his magnificent work.

Buried in the folds of the judge's bombast and exaggeration were several fine legal points: the sheriff's office was solely dependent on the *fees*—mileage fees and expense accounts—for reimbursement, and these were compiled by the sheriff himself who alone stood the expenses until reimbursed; train robbery was a crime of such serious nature that the Territorial Legislature had made it a capital offense; warrants for the arrest of the robbers were issued *within* the county. Therefore, having delivered his literature, the judge also rendered a verdict—in more mundane legal style: "The clerk is hereby directed to enter judgment for plaintiff for the sum of $2,285.20 and for costs of suit."

Unfortunately, a higher tribunal, the Territorial Supreme Court, received the case on appeal and, apparently having no taste for Walter Scott, Roderic Dhu, or Robin Hood, and certainly none for setting a precedent on costly out-of-county pursuits by lawmen, overturned the verdict. Buckey was left holding the bag for more than two thousand dollars plus court costs.

Of some possible balm to the judge, whose efforts in Buckey's behalf were far above the ordinary call of duty and seemingly correct, was a rather extraordinary coincidence in his use in his summation of the term "rough riders." If the judge lived to see it, Buckey O'Neill would contribute a great deal toward making that felicitous phrase famous 8½ years hence.

Ironically, J. J. Smith, although his sentence was longer than those of the other Diablo Canyon bandits, was to serve the shortest term. Smith won his release on August 13, 1893, having served only four of the thirty years. Next to be freed was Dan Harvick, on Christmas Day, 1896, after serving seven years. John Halford and William Sterin received their discharge from Yuma Prison on November 1, 1897, after completing eight years of their twenty-five-year sentences. Halford, it is believed, died in El Paso, Texas, of tuberculosis—the "prison plague"—a short time after his release.

Sterin, legend has it, enlisted in the First U.S. Volunteer Cavalry Regiment in the spring of 1898, under an assumed name. He is reputed to have been killed in the Battle of San Juan Hill.

CHAPTER FOURTEEN

Calamity on Walnut Creek

THE DIABLO CANYON case, once completed, proved to Buckey that the Yavapai County Sheriff's Office called for full-time effort—and then some. Accordingly, he suspended publication of *Hoof and Horn* in 1889, as if to trim back some of the frenetic activity that kept him from his writing and reading and hindered his political plans.

Yavapai County was outsized. Originally as large as the state of New York, it yielded, through acts of various legislatures, other counties such as Maricopa, Gila, Coconino, and Apache, but still remained large itself. The sheriff could spend little time shuffling papers and memorizing wanted posters; he spent his hours on horseback traveling the countryside, in which no mining camp or town seemed closer than fifty miles from another settlement.

In mid-July, the day after a Whiskey Row fire had threatened to level Prescott, and at about the time the former Hashknife waddies were being escorted to Yuma prison, Buckey received a note from a local character named A. W. "Old Grizzly" Callen. Callen, a placer miner at Oro Fino at the Placeritas diggings on the northeast tip of the Weaver Mountains, laconically stated in the note that he had killed two men invading his claim and was willing to give himself up to the law. "Old Grizzly" had come to Yavapai County in 1873 in a wagon train from Kansas, and was well known in Prescott as a hard-scrabbler who barely eked out wages on his claim but who generally was peaceful and unassuming.

Buckey, harboring no doubts that the grimy little note told the truth, rode the eighty-five miles to Callen's camp to take him into custody. The two dead men, Buckey learned, were Byron J. Charles and Frank Work, who jointly had owned a claim near Callen's. Old Grizzly told his story straight and without flourishes. Charles and Work had tried to force him to sign a fraudulent deed to his property, turning it over to them, he related. When they had come to his camp, armed and threatening his life, he had loaded his shotgun with coarse buckshot and cut each man in two with well-aimed shots.

Buckey took Callen back to the county jail at Prescott and recorded his statement. Claim jumpers were frowned upon in Arizona as much as horse thieves and cattle rustlers. As often as not, such mining-camp vermin were unceremoniously killed and buried in shallow graves and no one knew the difference. Old Grizzly's forthright confession was almost a novelty; the grand jury had no trouble finding him not guilty by reason of self-defense.

Mining camps were a never-ending source of business for the sheriff, although, fortunately, not many of the disputes reported emulated Old Grizzly Callen's solution. Nevertheless, isolated men, who were well acquainted with greed, jealousy, and whiskey, produced plenty of explosive situations. During Buckey's two-year hitch as sheriff, however, the greatest mining camp calamity was not a miner's feud, but one of the Territory's worst natural disasters. The Walnut Creek tragedy proved once again Buckey's eerie, lifelong proclivity for being near when bad news was happening.

In mid-February, 1890, it began to rain in the Prescott area —normally a welcome event. But this time water fell in blinding sheets without let-up, turning every dry wash, ravine, gully, and creek into a boiling torrent, brown with suspended mud, and churning with uprooted trees and dislodged boulders. Every street and trail became a sloppy gumbo, as the rain drummed frightfully against roof and window, keeping all but the most hardy indoors. After a week of the ceaseless downpour, reports

began filtering in from the Hassayampa Creek area south of
Prescott that the Walnut Creek Dam was showing signs of weak-
ening.

The dam, built in 1887 by a New York mining syndicate to
impound water for washing gravel and driving placer machinery, surrounded a mining camp in a narrow canyon of the Hassayampa Creek, in the Weaver District between Antelope Hill
and Wickenburg. It seemed sturdy enough; its 2½-foot-thick
walls, tapering upward from a broad base, were filled with
earth and rocks. The dam's construction had changed the map
in the area by forming a 1100-acre lake, about 60 feet deep,
some 2½ miles long, and ¾ mile wide. In times of normal
weather, Walnut Creek Dam and its lake had a picture-post-
card appearance of tranquil beauty. The lake, surrounded by
cottonwood and pine trees, had been stocked with fish and was
a favorite boating, canoeing, picnicking, and fishing resort. But
it soon would be only a memory.

By February 20, every creek, feeder, and finger tributary of
the Hassayampa—colorful little waterways with names like
Blind Indian, Milk Creek, Asastra, and Minneha—had turned
into a frothing monster. Each one poured its load of water, mud,
rock, brush, and trees into the Hassayampa, which in turn
slammed the load against the dam, pouring the excess over
the lip. Placer miners and squatters in the Hassayampa area
were warned to move to higher ground and some did; others
remained despite the desperate reports and entreaties of those
who felt the dam could not long hold back its mammoth load.
Buckey, rounding up every available man to survey the stricken
creek area, became convinced that only a miracle—specifically
a sudden abatement of the torrential rains—could prevent a
major disaster.

But the downpour did not stop. A few minutes before midnight on February 22, the ninth day of rain, the dam burst,
collapsing in a rubble swept instantly forward by the freed
water. Some recalled the mournful "whooshing" sound of the
pent-up water, as it broke loose with its load of debris. This

irresistible wall, 20 feet high, hurtled down the narrow canyon, leaving an unspeakable scene of destruction and desolation in its path. It inundated every flat piece of ground, pounding cabins and lean-tos and wooden mine trestles to match sticks, uprooting more trees and shoving ten-ton boulders from centuries-old perches. One mining camp known to have a population of 150 miners and their families disappeared in the mile-wide torrent as it rushed down to the town of Wickenburg, where it spread out in the mesquite thickets.

The day after the Walnut Creek dam disintegrated, the rains abated, permitting relief parties to enter the area to care for survivors, set up first-aid and food stations, and search for the dead. When news of the dam collapse reached him in Prescott, Buckey rushed to join the searchers who, in the days that followed, found fifty-six bodies floating in the death-dealing waters. Coffins were knocked together on the site and the bloated dead kept from view until they could be taken to Wickenburg and Prescott for burial. The hollow-eyed mining families, trembling lost children, weary and bedraggled relief workers, the crazy tangles of jetsam, the sputtering and flickering campfires, formed a grim tableau long to be remembered with a shudder of sadness.

On February 24, the *Prescott Journal-Miner*'s reporter on the scene quoted Sheriff O'Neill as saying, "The scene of desolation along the Hassayampa beggers description. A tornado could not have made such a complete wreck." The *Mohave Miner* said Sheriff O'Neill "stayed with the relief team day and night, caring for the living and burying the dead."

Buckey and the other searchers continued to comb the stricken area until the end of February but the last of the dead, or in some cases, traces of the dead, were to turn up weeks afterward. Down near Wickenburg, where the flood had eddied back into the mesquite brush, several Chinese queues were found tangled in the thorny bushes, grisly remnants of scalp still attached. It was reasoned that the Chinese drowning victims had been carried along by the flood until their hair caught in the debris, and their bodies were jerked free, leaving scalp and hair behind.

The terrible event of February 22 was long remembered in Yavapai County. For years afterward, the flood was used as a convenient conversational explanation for the question, "I wonder what ever became of old so-and-so?" The common response: "Well, I guess he went down the river."

One acquaintance Buckey made during the hectic relief work along the Hassayampa was a lanky New York-born West Point graduate named Alexander Oswald Brodie, who had been an engineer and superintendent on the Walnut Creek Dam project. Brodie's somewhat erratic career in the Army had included scouting for General Crook in the Tonto Basin area and service against the Nez Percé Indians in Idaho. The two men had much in common, not the least of which was a mutual interest in the military life. On Brodie's part this took the form of a yearning to get back to it; on Buckey's a yearning to make something of his new duties as adjutant general of Arizona Territory.

Buckey had received the title soon after his return to Prescott with the Diablo Canyon bandits. Governor Lewis Wolfley, the Territory's eighth governor and the man who had issued a highly congratulatory telegram to Sheriff O'Neill when he arrested the Hashknife cowboys in Utah, probably appointed Buckey to the post out of admiration for his quick apprehension of the A. and P. robbers. The smartness of the Prescott Grays under Buckey's captaincy also may have been a factor.

Being adjutant general of the Arizona militia was almost purely honorary, Buckey had found. In 1889, the U.S. Government appropriation to the National Guard of the several states and territories amounted to $400,000 but Arizona received nothing. As one newspaper pointed out soon after Buckey's appointment, "New Mexico gets $3501 and the other territories receive various sums ranging from $2847 to twice that amount. Even far away Alaska gets $3501. There is no good reason why the militia of Arizona should not be thoroughly organized and be made to form a part of the National Guard and participate

in the favors of the general government. The effort is worthy
of the attention of Adjutant General O'Neill."

The trouble with it all was that Buckey had no time. Governor Wolfley resigned on August 20, 1890, and was replaced
by John N. Irwin, who had been governor of Idaho in 1883.
Governor Irwin, taking office in January, 1891, had his own appointments to make. One of them was the new adjutant general.

Buckey's brief stint in the office ended after he had applied
to the U.S. secretary of war for permission to enlist a battalion
of troops from the militia organizations in the Territory to participate in the Sioux wars, either as infantry or cavalry. Washington rejected the idea.

In 1891, Alexander O. Brodie, who seven years later would
team up with his predecessor on a highly important military
matter, became the first commander of the Arizona National
Guard.

CHAPTER FIFTEEN

A Tax for the Iniquitous Railroad

DESPITE RUMORS that the railroad had engi-
neered an eleventh-hour ballot-box stuffing attempt against sheriff's candidate O'Neill, the
Atlantic and Pacific seemed grateful for the quick apprehension and punishment of the Diablo Canyon boys. The railroad
was only too glad to pay its reward to Buckey and his possemen,
and Buckey was only too glad to get his share. The sheriff's job,
while it could be good paying if a man rode a lot and collected
his mileage and expenses, greatly depended on rewards and
fines. But if there appeared to be a semblance of friendliness
between the sheriff and the railroad on completion of the Diablo
Canyon case, it quickly disappeared when the sheriff turned to
his duties as tax assessor-collector.

Buckey had made only one real campaign promise while
stumping the county in the fall of 1889: that, if elected, he
would exercise his responsibility as ex officio tax assessor to put
the bite on the mighty Atlantic and Pacific for the full value
of its land holdings in Yavapai County. At the time, no one
paid much attention to this idea; fewer still realized how revolutionary and windmill-tilting it would be; and probably no one
thought he actually would make a stab at it.

He did, though, and the "stab" took the form of one of
Buckey's famous letters—closely reasoned, statistic-filled pages
—sent to the Territorial Board of Equalization in Tucson. A
copy of the letter went to the Board's home office in Phoenix,
as well as to several key territorial newspapers. Buckey closed

all possible avenues of escape. He wanted his argument to be heard—and it was not only heard but repeated, echoing down the remotest outposts of the Territory for a long time to come, harvesting political hay as it went.

Buckey's letter took the form of a protest against the board's reduction of his assessment of the A. and P.'s "grant lands" in Yavapai County—a stunning 614,529 acres which Sheriff-Tax Assessor O'Neill valued at $1.25 per acre for a total "bill" of $892,260.38. Buckey took care to point out that the railroad's grant holdings in the county actually amounted to 4,280,578 acres; the lesser acreage represented that of which the company officially had "taken possession."

The letter was filled with sensible—particularly to the average taxpayer—arguments: Why, Buckey asked, should the railroad's assessment of a mere $1.25 per acre be reduced to a paltry 30 cents when private landowners were forced to pay $1.52 for each acre in their possession? And why should Yavapai County have to suffer the loss in tax revenues rightly due it, particularly when the land being assessed amounted to only a fraction of the railroad's actual holdings?

Buckey drove home a key point when he wrote:

... the 614,529 acres which were assessed by the assessor at $1.25 an acre, and reduced by the County Board of Equilization to thirty cents per acre, consist of some of the most valuable land in the Territory, being so heavily timbered that thousands and thousands of acres will yield from $50 to $100 in timber per acre, while not an acre of it can probably today be purchased for the $1.25 at which it was originally assessed. In fact, out of the millions of acres included within the Atlantic and Pacific Railroad grant, this 614,529 acres were selected because they were pre-eminently the most valuable—either by reason of their timber, their great adaptibility to agriculture, or for the control of valuable water privileges that their possession ensured.

To the man unlettered in the complications of taxation, pay-offs, coercion, and political favors, Buckey's final sentence in the above argument bore special impact. Hell, the sheriff was giving the railroad every benefit of the doubt—he was taxing them on only a little piece of their holdings! Buckey wrote:

And the valuation of $1.25 per acre placed on them by the assessor
was based not so much on their real value. as in the belief that by
making the valuation purposely so low that it would not only be
allowed to remain, but would be enforced by the proper authorities.

It is quite obvious from Buckey's extraordinary letter that the
political turnabout he was contemplating was imminent. Nothing 'is more clearly defined in his well-researched and cogent
argument than the burgeoning philosophy of the Populist.

Was it fair, he asked, to assess privately owned land $1.52 an
acre plus an additional sum for "improvements," and assess the
railroad for thirty cents on the acre when much of its land
lay side by side with private acreage—and not a cent for improvements? "Could anything be more unjust or iniquitous,"
he asked, "and still keep within the limits of the law" than the
railroad's game of "taking possession" over a fraction of its land
grant holdings, and paying a pittance in taxes on it, but at the
same time exercising control over all the remaining millions of
acres on which it was taxed not a cent?

Since this system of tax-evasion has been perfected by the railroad
company, it has not attempted to secure title to any more of its grant
lands, and why should it when the system ensures to it and those who
hold under it all the privileges of ownership with none of the burdens?

Buckey brought his letter to a close by calling on the territorial board to right an "injustice." It was a neat summing up:

Trusting that your Honorable Board will realize and correct this
injustice of making the resident owners in Yavapai County of 139,274
acres of land pay more than double the taxes paid by foreign corporations owning 713,808 acres in every way similar, and hoping that
you will see fit to re-establish the assessment against "grant" lands as
originally made by the assessor of Yavapai County, in justice to the
Territory and County who are alike injured through the diminution
of their revenues entailed by such a reduction.

The "injustice" of the railroad landowners, and the "foreign
corporations" involved in railroad ownership comprised two of
Populism's cardinal protests.

If Buckey blunted his lance in his tilting the A. and P. iron windmill, he must have realized he could make only a dent in the railroad's armor, not a hole. But one thing he did accomplish was to win the hearts of those who saw the issue as a battle of the common man against the "company"—the trust, the combine, the monopoly.

As for the railroad, the thirty-cent assessment stood for the time being but the A. and P. was forced into the uncomfortable necessity of taking the case through the courts.

Buckey, philosophically, was splitting from the Republican Party. He knew it and the Yavapai County Republican Party sensed it. Still, when the territorial convention was set for August 26, 1890, in Phoenix, the Yavapai County Republican Central Committee selected Buckey among the six delegates from Prescott.

CHAPTER SIXTEEN

Onyx, Silver, and Copper

ALTHOUGH THE Prescott countryside swarmed with miners and the hillsides were speckled with tailings and dump, Buckey O'Neill was no prospector. Speculator, perhaps, and certainly interested in mining, in the prospector's siren song of finding a mother lode or getting moderately rich from a lucky claim, Buckey was not a laboring man in the back-breaking, grubbing sense. It must have been seen as supremely ironic, therefore, that when Sheriff O'Neill decided to take a small plunge as a mine investor, he gave new meaning to the old saw about "the luck of the Irish."

Not long after the Walnut Creek Dam disaster, Buckey purchased a third share of 40 acres of land in one of the oldest mining areas in the Territory, some 28 miles south of Prescott at Mayer's Station, on Big Bug Creek. As a "mining" venture, the investment was somewhat smaller than a go-for-broke, Schieffelin-like affair. In fact, the "mine" was a marble quarry. Buckey, who paid $150 for his ⅓ share, was told it contained enough high-grade marble to make quarrying profitable, on a modest scale. Offered the remaining two shares for $300, he decided to let someone else "share the wealth."

The old saying about the man who fell into a Chick Sale and came out odoriferous of roses fit Buckey O'Neill to a tee. The marble quarry, it was learned once the blasting began, contained a horizontal ledge, 12 to 20 feet thick and 1,200 feet long, of pure "Mexican" onyx. The stone ran in variegated colors ranging from red, green, blue, gold, pink, white, and black to delicately translucent hues. Those who knew about such things

said it was the richest deposit of onyx between Prescott and
Puebla, Mexico, where the stone brought prices ranging from
$8 to $20 a cubic foot.

Samples of the various colors were sent to Chicago for careful
and expert assay. One newspaper, reaching an apogee of
wonderment about the onyx mine when the report came back,
commented: "Its value cannot be computed [even] by mathe-
maticians who do not care how many figures they use."

Actually, a mathematician would have come close to Buckey's
profit in the venture with a figure something like $67,000—a
sum that could easily cause a man to be called "rich" in Arizona
Territory in 1890.

In March, 1893, Buckey and his partners sold their interests
in the onyx quarry to "a party of eastern capitalists." The sale
was made in Los Angeles, said a newspaper report, "and the
consideration is said to have been $200,000. This is one of the
most valuable properties of the kind known."

Years later, Buckey's friend Jim McClintock said of him in a
speech, "Despite the fact that he gave away his loose cash to
any cowboy or prospector who asked, O'Neill became wealthy
. . . through the sale of an onyx mine near Big Bug." McClintock's evaluation of both Buckey's generosity and later wealth
from the mine sale cannot be doubted. McClintock himself, in
hard times, always could call upon his friend for a loan. He
never hesitated to do so, was never refused, and never failed
to pay it back.

Buckey decided some time in 1890—perhaps during his tussle
with the Atlantic and Pacific over its tax assessment—that he
would not seek reelection as sheriff. His political career had
reached a serious watershed, he felt, and the times seemed to
call for more than blind obedience to what appeared to be two
hack-ridden political parties. New ideas were in the air—free
silver, the single tax, Populism—and badly needed change
seemed to be in the offing.

The 1890 fall campaign for various local, county, and territorial offices had been a lackluster affair, particularly for the

Republicans, and Buckey had played little part in it. In fact, in the spring of 1891, when it was all over, he was charged with sabotaging some of the Republican campaign efforts. Buckey's response was typically meaty and belligerently defensive, but, at the base, it was a fabrication.

The *Arizona Republican* made the charge against Buckey on May 23, 1891, alleging "that the Catholics of a class, took part in the late political campaign in and around Prescott and against the Republican ticket. Among the active workers, and strange as it may appear, was General W. O. O'Neill, late Adjutant General."

Buckey answered in an "open letter," dated May 25 at Prescott, to the editor of the *Republican*. The former sheriff (he had relinquished the office the previous January) countercharged that the *Republican* was "conceived in the arrogant egotism of a coterie of self-constituted leaders." Asserting that the newspaper was supposed to be the "ten commandments of the Republican faith in Arizona," he observed that instead of a Messiah it had turned out to be a Mahdi.[6] In conclusion, he wrote: "As a Republican—one who loves the party, its principles and its glory—I protest against your attempt to identify me [with] the party which you assume to represent with such bigotry and intolerance."

For sound and fury, the statement could have received high marks; for significance and truth, zero.

Before taking another running plunge into the political waters, however, Buckey was drawn back to a project long in his thoughts: "development" of the Grand Canyon.

The canyon, with its sublime beauty, untrammeled vastness, and primitive history, captivated his imagination. He talked about it to Pauline in ecstatic terms but found he could not

6 Reference to a "Mahdi" may be somewhat obscure today, but it points up Buckey's preoccupation with military news of the day. The Mahdi, a self-proclaimed "chosen one," or messiah, rose to power in the Sudan in 1881, wresting the enormous African territory from Anglo-Egyptian control. General "Chinese" Gordon, the British mystic-soldier, died in the Sudanese city of Khartoum in 1885 after a siege by Mahdist fanatics, called "dervishes," and by the British soldier "Fuzzy-Wuzzies."

begin to put into words its absolutely cosmic quality; he considered it a marvel that should be known to every American, a true wonder of the world.

Of several germinal ideas he formed about the canyon, the main one had to do with establishing a scenic route to its South Rim to draw visitors from every state in the Union. Toward this end, Buckey enlisted Jim McClintock's help, and the two veteran newspapermen wrote letters to Eastern journals and to several of McClintock's influential friends on both coasts, touting the canyon and its unsurpassed potential for investment.

Buckey also invested in the canyon himself, becoming a partner in copper mining on the Coconino Plateau near the South Rim. For a time, in fact, he carried the somewhat burdensome title of "vice-president and general manager of the Grand Canyon Mining Company." The mining venture, unlike the onyx quarry on Big Bug Creek, petered out quickly. Geologists and mine experts found the copper deposits in limestone cappings with no continuous ledges or deposits of appreciable size, and none worth exploiting.

Buckey in his cabin in the Grand Canyon (Sharlot Hall Museum).

A third idea Buckey developed had great ramifications. The scenic route he envisoned became a reality when a spur rail line was built from Williams, thirty-five miles west of Flagstaff, to the Anita Mine. Later the Santa Fe took over this auxiliary line and extended it on to the South Rim. It was the beginning of the opening of the canyon to the world.

Some claimed Buckey's decision to bolt the Republican Party in 1892 was provoked by the party's attitude toward Mormonism. Since he belonged to a religious minority himself, there could be some truth in the observation. He followed closely the activities of the Sixteenth Legislative Assembly—which carved Coconino County out of the northern part of Yavapai—as it bogged down in attempting to frame a constitution to be submitted in a bid for statehood. One paramount issue at the Phoenix assembly in the fall of 1891, among the Republicans in particular, was the question of the "Idaho Test Oath," directed at Arizona's estimated twelve thousand Mormons. Buckey's party considered the Mormons' block of votes—set against some seventy thousand eligible voters in the territorial population— as pivotal, since they nearly always voted Democratic. Republican delegates argued strongly for inclusion in the constitution of the "oath," which would disenfranchise any Mormon who refused to denounce polygamy. Although the constitutional convention refused to include the test oath provision in its final draft, the fact that a faction had tried to push it through was no doubt bitter experience for Buckey.

But perhaps more weighty in his decision to renounce his party was his increasing alienation from the party bosses— notably Governor N. O. Murphy—and Buckey's increasing devotion to the tenets of Populism, particularly on the issue of the free coinage of silver.

Reduced to its simplest terms, Buckey simply did not believe that either national party, regardless of its free-silver support, had the interest of "the masses" at heart. He knew that, at the 1891 constitutional convention in Phoenix, the delegates had adopted a free-silver section calling for the equal footing of both gold and silver as legal tender in the Territory. He knew also that the author of the silver section was the Territory's delegate to Congress, Marcus Aurelius Smith. A staunch Democrat, Smith had issued a public statement, declaring, "I favor the reopening of our mints to the free coinage of silver and gold at a fixed ratio." And Buckey knew that the convention had adopted the silver section of its constitution with the full knowledge that, when presented to the Democrat "gold bug" president, Grover Cleveland, it would have about as much chance of survival as an icicle in Hell. It was not of any great moment, in Buckey's mind, that the Republican and Democratic parties (the latter as it reposed in Delegate Smith) favored free silver. It would hardly do *not* to support free silver in a silver-producing area. Buckey felt both parties were speaking out of both sides of their political mouths and were collectively guilty of deceit, corruption, gross bossism, and exploitation of the people.

Some, with long memories, recalling Buckey's five-hundred-dollar gouge of years past, his legal case to "add" two thousand dollars to his expenses in the Diablo Canyon case, and similar "peccadillos," felt his position a trifle heavy in sanctimony and not far removed from the pot-and-kettle analogy.

The issue of free coinage of silver happened to be the focus of third-partyism in the 1890's and Buckey, before he officially became a Populist, made two significant statements on the silver question. In a long and rather turgid discourse published in the *Arizona Weekly Enterprise* of Tucson, he wrote:

The destruction of silver is but the forging of another link in the chain to enfetter the borrowing classes. There are but two parties—the anti-silver and the silver party—the party of the money lender and the party of the people. One represents the strengthening of the moneyed power of the nation, the other is fighting against the further peonage of the masses. On one side is arrayed the power of the administration, its offices, its honors and its emoluments, aided and abetted by the money-loving wing of the republican party. On the other, a few men whose only strength is that of justice and right—

who have neither place nor pelf with which to buy or influence the votes of their colleagues.

In this statement, made just before he decided that neither national party quite fit the "party of the people" label, Buckey correctly predicted, "There is no doubt but what the result will be the repeal of the Sherman Act." This act, passed in 1890, provided that the U.S. government would purchase each month 4,500,000 ounces of silver and issue against it paper notes that would be legal tender and redeemable in either gold or silver coin at the discretion of the secretary of the Treasury. The Sherman Act was pure manna to silver-producing regions and at least a compromise of sorts for those who favored "the free and unlimited coinage of silver." But Buckey had nailed it right. The Sherman Act was repealed late in 1893 and silver in Arizona Territory dropped from $1.25 to as low as 25 cents an ounce. As a result, mines closed all over the Territory, as well as throughout the West.

When, on July 4, 1893, a convention of "free silverites" gathered in Silver City, New Mexico, Buckey was in attendance, along with silver men of both major parties and a number of lesser ones. Buckey, feeling no great admiration for the convention's empty rhetoric, wrote about it in the *Arizona Weekly Enterprise* two weeks after it closed. Of the resolutions passed, he said: "The greatest 'gold bug' that ever lived can read them with as much satisfaction as the men who framed them." He then went on to solidify his personal decision to adopt Populism as his political credo:

While this convention of democratic and republican delegates was in session, one hundred and fifty thousand men were crowding the western states and territories seeking the work that the closing down of the silver mines had taken from them.

Today the interests of the west are prostrated and chilled into death by commercial stagnation through the policy of these two parties.

Those reading into Buckey's free-silver statements the squirming of a man about to run for office made a mental note of

Buckey's reference to "these *two* parties," and of the *Tucson Enterprise's* charge that he had tried to sabotage his party in the 1890 campaign. An additional gleeful note was made of the other pot of hot water Buckey fell into toward the close of 1893.

Arizona Territory, particularly since it was seeking statehood perennially, was greatly interested in making an impression at the Chicago Columbian Exposition set for the 400th anniversary of the discovery of America (actually the 401st). The queen of Spain was sending replicas of Columbus' ships, *Niña, Pinta,* and *Santa María*; Alexander Graham Bell was to open a telephone line between Chicago and New York; millions were expected to travel from the four corners of the country— indeed the world—to see the marvelous buildings, inventions, displays, and exhibits. The City of Prescott issued $30,000 in bonds for its Chicago exhibit, and Buckey was appointed to head the commission to escort to Illinois materials for the first "general" display of Arizona products, especially of agricultural and mining industries ever shown outside the Territory.

On November 14, 1892, apparently in disagreement with members of the special World's Fair Commission appointed by Governor John N. Irwin, Buckey resigned as president of the Prescott delegation. The *Arizona Gazette* in Phoenix published a story on the resignation the following August and dropped a bombshell: it implicated Buckey in mismanagement of the $30,000 World's Fair monies subscribed in Prescott. The *Gazette* claimed to be reporting charges made by the World's Fair managers themselves.

Buckey responded through the pages of the *Arizona Republican.* The Phoenix paper, at least partially owned by Republican Party boss Oakes Murphy, ordinarily was Buckey's strongest rival. Buckey claimed he had frittered away no funds and what money he had spent, a little over $2,900, had been for "defraying expenses for advertising, printing, salary of secretaries, sale of bonds, and collecting of county exhibits," and that upon his resignation from the Prescott delegation on November 4, 1892, the balance remaining was $27,096.69.

A very damaging rejoinder to Buckey's statement came from one George F. Coates of Chicago, representing the Board of World's Fair Managers. Coates, who appeared to have done an extraordinary amount of research—even learning that Buckey had been publishing a few of his fiction pieces in San Francisco newspapers—responded in the *Republican* six weeks after Buckey's explanation, saying the O'Neill account of the controversy

. . . reads like one of the gentlemen's articles, descriptive of strange men and impossible animals, written to fill space in the San Francisco newspapers at $10 per column. . . . The controversy is between Mr. O'Neill and the records, the former trying to show there was an expenditure of but $2903.31 provided for during his connection with the board as president, and the record showing the amount to be $13,837.32. . . .

Coates further stated that Buckey had resigned the post "because the board refused to appropriate $3000 to a scheme which they thought to be pushed by Mr. O'Neill's private interests." He added, somewhat coyly, that although Buckey "is prominently connected with the largest onyx claim in the territory, the only dressed and polished onyx in our exhibit are five slabs borrowed from parties in Chicago."

As it turned out, Buckey had strong ground to stand on and stood on it firmly. He pointed out that Governor Louis C. Hughes, secretary of the Fair Commission and successor to John Irwin, had acknowledged in a letter dated December 2, 1892, that the total amount of funds on hand at O'Neill's resignation was $27,096.69, the precise figure Buckey had quoted. Buckey let the matter drop, saying, "This is a controversy for Mr. Hughes and Mr. Coates to settle between them," but went on to give his impression of Arizona's contribution to the Chicago Exposition:

In its way the exhibit is unique. It is an exhibit that does not exhibit. With 20,000 square miles of timber lands there is not enough timber at the exhibit to kindle a fire. With 7,000 square miles of coal lands, according to the U.S. geological survey, a man might carry on his back all the coal that the exhibit contains. With three-quarters of a million acres of land irrigated by nearly five hundred miles of canal, there is not a peach, a pear, a plum or an apricot, an orange, a fig or a lemon to show that fruits grow in Arizona, or a spear of wheat or barley or alfalfa to show that a farmer exists in the territory.

In all, Buckey had undergone some serious scoring in newspapers in the period 1891-1893, and had accumulated a considerable number of enemies to offset the friends and allies earned in a dozen years' residence in the Territory. The following year, 1894, promised to be one of at least equal interest; it was an election year, and Buckey was determined to test the political waters once again, if for no other reason than to find out how cold they would be to a Populist's toe.

CHAPTER SEVENTEEN

J'Accuse: The Populist Candidate of 1894

OF ALL THE SEVERAL forces that drove Buckey O'Neill from the Arizona Republican Party ranks in 1894, probably none tipped the scales more than his rift with the party's bosses, particularly the Murphy brothers, Nathan Oakes and Frank.

Oakes Murphy loomed as powerful as his name in the Territory's turn-of-the-century politics. Born in Maine in 1849, he would have the distinction of being the only man selected twice to serve as governor of the Territory.[7] Frank, his older brother, was a prominent businessman in the northern part of the Territory, engaged in mining ventures, a Prescott mercantile company, and railroading. Separately or together, the Murphys were respected as formidable Republican Party bosses.

Oakes, who as President Benjamin Harrison's nominee, became governor in 1892, espoused some seemingly progressive ideas: high taxation of liquor to regulate the sale of intoxicants and "improve the character" of saloons; repeal of laws governing licensing of gambling houses in favor of local options; and the passage of a law granting the voting franchise to women. But Governor Murphy also favored exempting new railroads from taxation. He considered new rail ventures highly risky business that ought to be offered inducements instead of being penalized. Accordingly, the Seventeenth Legislative Assembly exempted new railroads from taxation and did nothing to reassess further the enormous railroad land holdings already granted.

[7] Murphy served in 1892–1893 and 1898–1902.

Buckey considered this obsequiousness toward the rail lines a personal slap in the face. As Yavapai County tax assessor-collector he had made a spirited attempt to assess the Atlantic and Pacific for only a portion of the taxes he felt the line legitimately owed, and had been beaten down as a result. Now his own party was upholding the "iniquitous" tax evasion scheme he had sought to thwart. To Buckey, the whole business abused the ordinary taxpayer and was a fawning case of flagrant favoritism.

In April, 1893, the governorship once again changed hands. Oakes Murphy, Harrison's Republican nominee, was replaced by Louis C. Hughes, a Grover Cleveland Democrat. Governor Hughes, a diminutive newspaper owner with a clergyman's air and forbidding appearance, was well-meaning. A teetotaler, he opposed licensed liquor and gambling, claiming that three-fourths of the inmates at the Yuma Territorial Prison and half the residents of the Phoenix insane asylum were there as a result of "intemperance." The Territory's 635 saloons, he believed, lay at the root of many of Arizona's crime and violence problems. In vain, he pleaded for fair taxation of land properties, regardless of special-interest ownership.

President Cleveland's choice of Hughes to replace Oakes Murphy effected a split in Arizona's Democratic Party ranks. The Territory's Democratic Central Committee opposed the nomination, as did the Arizona delegate to Congress Marcus A. Smith. The rift among Hughes's supporters and detractors boded ill for the Democrats in the 1894 elections.

Several writers have made the claim that former Governor Murphy, still the Republican kingpin in Arizona, and his brother Frank offered Buckey O'Neill the party's nomination as delegate to Congress if he would "lay off" the railroads. This meant not pushing for federal legislation requiring survey of railroad-controlled lands, a measure that would insure their being placed on tax rolls. Such an offer may have been made, though it seems unlikely, since Oakes Murphy was planning to seek the nomination himself.

In any case, Buckey had no intention of making deals with Republican bosses. By 1893 he was a full-fledged Populist, in philosophy and in fact.

For a movement that survived a bare half-dozen years, Populism—the philosophy of the People's Party—carved one of the most curiously progressive, farsighted, and influential chapters in American political history. Its period of effective existence was limited to the period 1890-1896. For all intents and purposes, it died out with William McKinley's victory over William Jennings Bryan in the 1896 presidential election, but its impact on political thought continued to be heard and felt and practiced, its cardinal tenets realized, long after the "Pops" were forgotten.

The People's Party was blessed—or perhaps cursed—with some of the most flamboyant political leaders ever: Tom Watson of Georgia, the movement's chief demagogue and father figure; Congressman "Sockless" Jerry Simpson, the Socrates of Kansas; Jacob "Good Roads" Coxey of Massillon, Ohio, who would gather an "army" and march on Washington in 1894; Mary Ellen Lease, the "Kansas Pythoness" who advised Kansas farmers to "raise less corn and more hell"; and Ignatius Donnelly of Minnesota, champion of the Baconian Theory and chronicler of the Lost Continent of Atlantis.

But for all the attraction the Populist movement seemed to have for the square peg, it began to show its strength in the 1892 national elections when it nominated General James B. Weaver. A former Greenbacker from Iowa, Weaver polled more than a million popular votes, carried four states, and won twenty-two electoral votes for an impressive third-party showing.

The People's Party, despite the scarifying charges against it, unfolded as a natural phenomenon in a time of great social, economic, and political discontent in America. Mark Sullivan, newspaperman and historian of the era, listed several of the chief causes for this unrest, noting such developments as the end of free land distribution in the country, the increase in population out of proportion to the increase in the gold supply, the oppressive practices of railroads, the rise of trusts and monopolies, the power of organized wealth in politics, immigration, and the rise of labor unions.

The Populists offered solutions and relief for many of these problems. In so doing they attracted support in such unlikely places as Arizona Territory, political boomerang of the two national political parties, and in such ripe-for-change politicians as William Owen O'Neill.

Populism began as an agrarian movement devoted to the complaints of the nation's farmers. This group was fearful that the country's old agrarian society—symbolized in Thomas Jefferson's "sturdy yeoman"—was being battered out of existence by disproportionate taxes on farm land and a host of malevolent forces spreading from the industrial East to the agricultural South, Middle West, and West. The Populist credo maintained that land held the source of all wealth and was the heritage of the people, not of special interests, the wealthy, or the government. Land, the People's Party felt, should not be doled out by the government as largesse for industry's favors but should be held for the use of the American people—particularly the farmer-settlers. Thus the Pops adamantly called for the federal government to recover lands granted to the railroads and other corporations in excess of their actual needs, and to prohibit alien ownership of such lands. Populism believed that the railroads, frivolously levying discriminatory rates, enjoyed far too much governmental favoritism, especially in the form of tax shelters at the expense of the private landowner. To relieve this situation, it advocated that the government control and regulate the railroads and telegraph companies as a means of ending the railroads' death grip on millions of square miles of untouchable land. At the same time, a death blow would be dealt to industrial monopoly, since trusts were built largely on transportation monopolies.

Small wonder that this heady brew, the crux and kernel of the Populist philosophy, drew Buckey O'Neill like a lodestone.

Populism also advocated other reforms: a flexible currency; an income tax to tap other forms of wealth and relieve pressures on land and farm taxation; a postal saving system as protection for depositors in small-town banks who ran the risk of disastrous losses in times of agricultural depression; the secret ballot, registration laws, direct primaries, women's suffrage, popular election of senators, limitations of presidential terms, the eight-hour working day, and immigration restriction.

The Populists in 1892 also endorsed a plank in their party platform calling for the free and unlimited coinage of silver at the ratio of sixteen to one. To those who saw the free-silver movement as a transitory issue, the flocking to its banner held ominous consequences for the Populist movement's future. Henry Demarest Lloyd, a leading reformer-author-socialist, for example, termed the free-silver hullabaloo "the cow-bird of the Reform movement," saying "It waited until the nest had been built by the sacrifices and labor of others and then laid its eggs in it, pushing out the others which lie smashed on the ground."

The man who had so fearlessly billed the Atlantic and Pacific Railroad for a fair share of Yavapai County's tax burdens, and who had spoken so eloquently on the free silver issue, was eagerly nominated by the 1894 Populist convention in Arizona to make the race for congressional delegate. Buckey's opponents were former Governor Nathan Oakes Murphy, on the Republican ticket, and Prescott Democrat John C. Herndon.

Despite obvious hostilities between Murphy and Buckey, the campaign did not heat until a month or so before election day. Buckey stumped the Territory in his typical all-stops-out fashion. He found far too few hours in the day to travel to the far-flung communities, particularly the isolated mining camps and small agricultural centers, which he knew held his best hope for Populist sympathies. Then, on October 12, he published a broadside, an "open letter" addressed to both Murphy and Herndon, in which he stated in eloquent terms not only why

Buckey the congressional candidate,
1894.

the Populist party had the right to exist, but also why the country's two major parties deserved to be defeated. The booklet amounted to Buckey O'Neill's "J'Accuse."

The "open letter" said, in part:

For the creation of a new party there can be but one excuse—the existence of corruption and evils in public affairs that older parties have either not the ability or the desire to eradicate.

When such evils become so intolerable and malignant as to threaten national life and liberty, and individual prosperity, political revolution is the highest patriotism. It is a duty to God and Country.

If by the rule of the Republican and Democratic parties one man may enjoy a heaven on earth, a hundred equally as free born suffer that hell born of want and oppression; if by the rule of these two parties the wine and light of life, its music and its mirth, shall be the part of a few, and its dregs and darkness, its sorrows and its misery, the portion of the many, then the People's Party is entitled to exist.

Buckey then turned to his opponents:

Your parties do not represent the American people. They represent merely organized wealth.

You have appealed to prejudice and not to reason . . . You have erected political idols which you would force all men to fall down and adore, and this fetish worship you are still preaching. While you preach, the political cars of Juggernaut crush the life out of our people, and you stand calmly by and proclaim that "all is well."

Now, with his personal Juggernaut rolling, Buckey rung in reference to one of the great cause célèbres of the day, the Homestead strike. In June, 1892, workers at Andrew Carnegie's Homestead steel mill near Pittsburgh refused a wage reduction offered by Carnegie's deputy, Henry Clay Frick. As a result, Frick locked the steelworkers out of the plant and hired Pinkerton guards to keep them out. Outraged, the workers captured the plant, driving out Pinkertons, nonstriking steel workers, and Carnegie officials. That which followed polarized the nation: Frick brought three hundred Pinkerton men up the Monongahela in a barge; the embattled strikers, fighting from behind makeshift barricades, used rocks, bullets and dynamite, old cannon, and even a flaming raft against "the Pinkerton Hessians." Casualties on both sides rose to ten dead and sixty-five wounded. The brutal affair lasted nearly five months, but the strike was broken when National Guardsmen permitted non-union workers to enter the mill and begin firing the steel furnaces.

Buckey continued:

You have seen Mr. Harrison call into the councils of national legislation Mr. Carnegie, that he might dictate the rate of tariff that the American people should be taxed on steel and iron, and you have seen the wives of Homestead made widows and their children orphans by the bullets of Pinkerton thugs in order that this man Carnegie might add to his wealth at the expense of American labor. . . . You know that this deification of gold means simply the enrichment of the money owning classes, and the improverishment and debasement of the masses.

To candidate O'Neill, the "open letter" represented a last-ditch effort. Greatly needing and desperately wanting to meet both Murphy and Herndon in public debate, he ended by issuing his challenge:

... that you may no longer betray the people of Arizona into blindly following in the way in which you have led them in the past, I now ask that you meet me on the stump before the people of Arizona, that they may judge between us. I ask it in the name of the men who have been driven from Arizona with their wives and children to seek new homes elsewhere. I ask it in the name of the deserted mining camps of Arizona—those silent graveyards of human effort and industry. I ask it in the name of those men of Arizona who are still our brethren; those women who are still our sisters. . . . I concede to you, gentlemen, the right to fix the time and place and terms—my only stipulation is that I shall meet the two of you at the one time. I demand this, for my fight is not with the Republican or the Democratic party alone—it is with both.

Neither Murphy nor Herndon was such a political novice as to take up the challenge. Buckey's only hope for a "showing" in the 1894 voting was the split in the Democratic ranks effected by President Cleveland's choice of Louis C. Hughes as the new territorial governor.

The split did indeed affect the voting outcome. The Democrats lost their delegate to Congress, an office held by Marcus A. Smith since 1886. Nathan Oakes Murphy, the former governor and Republican party wheelhorse, won Smith's chair in Washington, and William O. O'Neill of the People's Party made his showing. The tally: Murphy, 5,686; Herndon, 4,773; O'Neill, 3,006.

To place third in a field of three could be no great honor, no matter what the odds, but Buckey took some solace in the knowledge that he had no influential backing and no organization, represented a third party decried by the bulk of the Territory's newspapers as "radical" and "socialistic," and fought two well-oiled political machines in the bargain. For all that, a quarter of the votes cast was at least a showing.

CHAPTER EIGHTEEN

J'Accuse in Reverse:
The Populist Candidate of 1896

BUCKEY'S DEFEAT in the outlands of Arizona was offset by the victories of his adopted party. The 1894 elections increased the Populist vote by 42 percent over that garnered by General Weaver and other People's Party candidates 2 years previously. The party elected 4 senators, 4 representatives to Congress, 21 state officials, 150 state senators and 315 state representatives. Furthermore, the party's influence was increasing enormously. More and more candidates from the 2 major parties revealed strong Populist sympathies, and more and more Democrats and Republicans in public office were making noises that sounded familiarly like Populist noises.

With Populism becoming a force to be reckoned with, and with the assurance of his adopted party's officials in Arizona that they were entirely pleased with his performance in the delegate race, Buckey began to look forward to 1896.

But 1894 had exhausted him, and Buckey welcomed a chance to breathe the unpoliticized air of the Grand Canyon and of home, with Pauline, before regrouping for an even harder run toward Washington. He therefore needed no persuasion to aid a scientific expedition of the Smithsonian Institution when it came to him for help. He led the group into the prehistoric Montezuma's Castle cliff dwelling in Verde Valley south of Flagstaff, an area he knew as well as he knew the canyon. Besides being a refreshing change from politics, it gave him a chance to talk to important people—scientists, explorers, archae-ologists—about the natural wonders of Arizona, and to give them a message they, hopefully, would take back to Washington with their rock samples, bones, and maps.

Buckey's guiding the Smithsonian expedition contributed to the proclamation by the federal government in 1906 that later made the historically priceless Montezuma's Castle a national monument.

In July, 1895, Buckey demonstrated that, while feeling strongly that the major political parties were basically corrupt and unworthy of anything above polite disdain, he still could defend a just man, regardless of party label.

Louis Hughes, the Cleveland appointee who had succeeded Oakes Murphy as governor, fell quickly out of favor with the Cleveland administration. Inspectors from the Department of Interior built a case against the somewhat feckless Hughes, accusing him, among other things, of using "undue influence" with the legislature to secure passage of bills he favored. Clearly, though, the charge was trumped-up and meaningless; Hughes had run afoul of Cleveland administration policy by opposing disposition of lands Congress had granted Arizona for educational purposes. In defense of Hughes, Buckey addressed a letter to President Cleveland, saying:

> I deem it my duty to say in his behalf, that during his term of office Governor Hughes has given the Territory a clean and economic administration of public affairs, which is admitted and meets with the approval of all except those who are his personal enemies. While I know, from personal experience as a candidate for Congress in that Territory during the last campaign, that Governor Hughes' views on the "silver question" are not in accord with the great mass of citizens in Arizona—and while I am politically opposed to him, I honestly believe that his removal at this time in the face of the reforms he has brought about, would be an act of official prejudice.

For a saloon man of long and legendary experience to speak up so generously for a WCTU-supported teetotaler and liquor-gambling reformer was high praise indeed. Still, Hughes was removed in March, 1896, to be replaced by a more Clevelandish gold democrat, Benjamin Franklin.

Biennial elections allow little time for rest, relaxation, cave exploring, or much of anything else—as any U.S. congressman today can testify. Oakes Murphy had hardly taken his seat in Washington as the Territory's congressional delegate in January, 1895, when plans were laid to see that he didn't return there in January, 1897.

The coming elections of 1896 promised nothing so clearly as absolute repudiation of the policies of the incumbent President Grover Cleveland, even by his own party. Democrats felt that Cleveland had sold out to banking syndicates and monied interests of various sorts, and that he was operating "government by injunction," a term arising from his handling of the Pullman strike, by sending federal troops to Chicago. The most influential Democrats, moreover, were silver men; silver was the crusade, and the knight with the silver armor was a Bible-banging, golden-voiced orator from Nebraska named William Jennings Bryan.

When the Democrats convened in Chicago on July 7, 1896, Bryan was ready to make his bid for a place in history. He literally carried the convention into a kind of semireligious ecstasy with his magnificent peroration, carefully tuned and timed, and delivered with as splendid a set of vocal chords as God ever granted a man and capped with a masterful conclusion: "You shall not press down upon the brow of labor this crown of thorns, you shall not crucify mankind upon a cross of gold!" The pandemonium that followed Bryan's final chisled phrase was indicative of the amalgamation of people—and parties—who soon would flock to his silver banner.

The national convention of the People's Party began on July 22, an unbearably muggy season in St. Louis, and 1,400 keyed-up delegates broke out their palmetto fans in a futile effort to stir a breeze. Buckey, seeing the city of his birth for the first time as an adult, knew from the start, as did most delegates, that the hottest thing in the air was the word "fusion"—fusion of the Populists with the Democrats in support of Bryan.

Among the Populist hierarchy there existed vehement opposition to the move. Tom Watson of Georgia, for instance, viewed the idea as analogous to the Biblical tale of Jonah and the whale: "We play Jonah while they play whale," he said. Henry Demarest Lloyd sensed that Bryan, stripped of the silver panacea, was a conservative political hack who, if elected, would repudiate every Populist demand. And perhaps the strongest motive put forward for remaining free of the Democrats was the reiterated fear that Populism, once absorbed, would never again emerge as a free and independent political entity and spirit.

The Republican candidate was a harmless Canton, Ohio, lawyer and tariff expert named William McKinley, a faithful party man with six terms in Congress and two as governor of Ohio. With crafty engineering by McKinley's friend, confidant, and fellow Ohioan, Marcus Alonzo Hanna, the Republican convention in St. Louis, June 16-18, nominated McKinley on the first ballot.

The Populists simply had no other viable alternative except to "fuse" with the Democrats, Bryan, and free silver; so they did it, and the campaign got underway in July, as soon as the "Pops" returned home.

Buckey, running again for the congressional delegate's seat, was opposed on the Democratic side by the party's tried and true Marcus A. Smith. The Republicans came up with A. J. Doran of Yavapai County, president of the Eighteenth Legislative Assembly Council.

Writing of the 1896 campaign, Jim McClintock, Buckey's long-time friend and later an eminent historian of the Territory, commented:

The campaign he waged in 1896 for delegate to Congress was in many points the most notable in the annals of the Territory. He had practically to play a lone hand. He was the nominee of the Populists, but that party was poorly organized and ill-equipped with the sinews of war ... [he traveled] by long passes across deserts, malapai, mesas, and unbroken forests, secluded hamlets where the spellbinder was a stranger, a new critter. It is probable that during this unique tour Buckey saw at least ninety percent of the voters of the Territory. He had to meet the hostility of every important newspaper and all the big "interests" were ranged in opposition.

Of course visiting the secluded hamlets and crossing the mountain and mesa were not exactly new experiences for a man involved in his fourth political campaign. And in 1896 Bryan was doing about the same thing. The "Boy Orator of the Platte" traveled eighteen thousand miles, visited twenty-one states and made up to half a dozen speeches a day.

McClintock, in noting the hostility of the newspapers toward the O'Neill candidacy, neglected to specify that Buckey's Populism had cost him even the support of an old friend and political ally of long standing, the *Prescott Journal-Miner*. The *Miner*, being die-hard Republican, had vigorously supported Oakes Murphy both as governor and as delegate to Congress; it could not—or at least did not—continue its support of Buckey once he had bolted and excoriated the Republican Party.

The *Journal-Miner*, in fact, was responsible for a brutal anti-O'Neill full-page story that ran at the crest of the 1896 campaign as a sort of counter-J'Accuse on Buckey's "record" as office-holder and taxpayer. The story, widely reprinted, was headed in the *Arizona Stock-Journal*:

BUCKEY O'NEILL'S RECORD
Has Sucked $80,000 From
Yavapai County
Now Posing as the Friend of the
Dear People
Has Paid Eleven Dollars and Twenty
Cents a Year on an Average
in Taxes

The story began:

Buckey O'Neill has set himself up as the self constituted guardian of the taxpayers of Arizona, the sympathizing friend of the "toiling masses," the foe of capital and the friend of labor.

. . . from the sympathizing wails which emanate, both from pen and jaw, one would think that he was the taxpaying Atlas of Arizona, upon whose shoulders rested the whole financial structure of the territory. From the agonizing strains, in regard to labor and the oppression which he alleges it endures, one would think that he had gone down into the bowels of the earth and had snatched therefrom the rich and valuable treasures implanted there for the use of man; that he had delved in the soil in the burning heat of the sun, and, with nature's aid, compelled it to yield its products for his benefit and that of his fellow man. Such would be naturally the impression obtained from his utterances. But if he ever dug from the earth a pound of ore, or if he ever made two blades of grass grow where only one grew before, he has left no record of it.

The *Miner* continued to its point. In columns of figures, it revealed that Buckey, in his 14 years of residency in Yavapai County, had earned something like $80,000 from the county treasury. Furthermore, the newspaper alleged that during only 7 of those 14 years had Buckey's name appeared on the tax rolls and that he had paid, for the 7 years, an average of $11.27 per year on an aggregate property assessment of $5,259.

"Just think of the onerous burdens," the *Miner* jibed, "which have been imposed on this ambitious and aspiring statesman! Just think of the oppressions he has suffered during all these years! Why to be compelled to pay eleven dollars and twenty-seven cents a year, just for the privilege of living in Arizona, is enough to impel any man to run for Congress."

Picking up the pace and referring to Buckey as a "tax-eating, pap-sucking citizen," the *Miner* asked: "Is it incumbent on a man who preaches and advocates populism, and affects a sympathy for the taxpayer, that he must necessarily become a tax dodger?"

Cogently and carefully the *Miner* developed its case against Buckey like a prosecuting attorney, building a case against a criminal suspect, block by block. In a sea of print, occasionally broken up by a boxed sum of figures, the paper specified printing fees, pay for reporting, salary as probate judge, mileage, postage, telegrams, commission on licenses, fees, contingent ex-

penses, and salary as sheriff. The newspaper listed amounts
ranging from $10 for "court reporting" to $19,229.08 as "Total
for 1890 as sheriff etc." Leaving no loopholes, the *Miner* survey
went to great lengths to explain that a sheriff received considerable mileage fees in a county as large as Yavapai—which
then embraced all of Coconino and a portion of Gila County in
the Tonto Basin area—in the serving of papers in remote
corners of the jurisdiction, and in the handling of criminal and
civil cases as well.

Summing up, the paper came up with a figure of eighty
thousand dollars received "from the tax payers of Yavapai
County," in Buckey's fourteen-year residency, then asked:

Is there any one so obtuse of mental perception as to fail to compre-
hend, in the light of this record, where his great love for the taxpayers [lies]—just as the wolf loves the lamb, the hawk the chicken.
He loves to devour his substance.

In the face of this record, is there an unbiased and intelligent man,
who has the welfare of the territory at heart, who can accept his
present declarations as sincere, or who can conscientiously give their
support to him for the reasonable position of delegate to congress?

Is it not apparent to all that his present utterances are as sounding
brass and tinkling cymbals, simply the utterances of a political demagogue, who having lived for fourteen years as a parasite on the public,
desires still further to retain his hold on the public treasury?

The story was a bruising, relentless—indeed, brilliant—attack
which, one thinks with hindsight, probably could not have been
published without inside help in Prescott and the territorial
capital.

Perhaps fortunately for Buckey, the *Miner* accounting sheet
came late in the campaign, negating any need for a spirited response, countercharges and accusations, and the usual impedi-
menta of political in-fighting in the newspapers. That the ledger
sheet came from an avowedly Republican journal blunted its
effect to some extent, but Buckey was never able to gauge its
damage.

One thing about the attack that is fairly certain: it was em-
barrassingly accurate in its figures, with perhaps a small error

here and there. Not that there was anything illegal about it; it was simply embarrassing.

The Democrat's veteran Congressional delegate Marcus A. Smith breezed back into office when the returns were counted in November. The score: Smith, 6,065 votes; Doran, 4,049; O'Neill, 2,695.

No progress in two years; in fact, 311 votes lost somewhere along the way. There could be no comfort, this time, in small considerations such as the fact that Marcus Smith, going back to Washington for what was to be the first of 4 more terms, was a strong free-silver man. McKinley, campaigning from his front porch, had been elected president. Even if Smith had won by a scant half million popular votes out of the 14 million cast, he had won and Populism was bust.

CHAPTER NINETEEN

The Popular, Populist Mayor of Prescott

THROUGHOUT HIS CAREER in Arizona, Buckey kept in contact with his parents in Washington, mostly by correspondence. The trip eastward to the capital was arduously long by rail. On the few occasions that he did return, he tried to combine business with pleasure by taking along a chunk of onyx for assaying, or visiting in New York with a businessman friend, Thurlow Weed Barnes, who had been associated with Buckey in the copper mine and railroad promotions in Grand Canyon. On such trips he also visited in Washington with Captain John and Mary, brother and sister.

The year 1897 quickly brought great sadness for Buckey, as he received word on January 13 that his father had died at his home at 208 Ninth Street. Buckey and Pauline traveled to Washington to witness the captain's burial in Arlington National Cemetery. Captain O'Neill's death at age sixty-three was the result of the accumulated effects of the terrible wound he had received at Fredericksburg thirty-five years previously.

Returning to Prescott in February, Buckey fervently entered the contest for mayor. His two losing campaigns for the delegate's seat in Congress had left him weary but undaunted, certain that he had a political future in Arizona—even as a Populist and with one of his town's major newspapers still clucking over his tax record.

Buckey's sensitivity to the respect his own townspeople had for him was warranted. The 1897 race for the mayor's office was never even a contest; Buckey walked in without the slightest abrasion and with only token opposition.

The new mayor took office in mid-1897. Although some were saying he would use his easily won post as a ladder for another shot at the delegate's race a year later, he took over the job with his usual perfervidity, launching immediately into a number of knotty municipal problems. Prescott's municipal water system and land-tax reforms were two of the knottiest.

Like most of the more studious Populists, Buckey had become a devotee of the "single tax" theory of Henry George, whose famous book, *Progress and Poverty*, had been published in 1879, the year Buckey had settled in Arizona, and who had died while Buckey was running for the mayor's office. In essence, the book explored the singular phenomenon of the "increase of want" as a concomitant to the "increase of wealth." The former maliciously followed the latter, as someone described it, "like a hideous Siamese Twin." Henry George placed the blame for this situation on the premise that land, the source of all wealth, gained in value as civilization advanced and the added wealth, instead of benefiting all, went into the pockets of the landlords. As a solution to the problem, he proposed "the single tax," a governmental levy on the unearned increase in land values which he believed would result in an end to land speculation and a more just distribution of wealth.

Buckey felt that Prescott could benefit from George's theory and so helped push through the city council a tax reform proposal. He described it in a letter to Jim McClintock on July 14, 1897:

At the meeting of the City Council on Monday night last we adopted a tax law for the first time putting into operation in America the principles of the single tax. The tax established is two dollars per annum per lot, the idea being to abolish licenses, and to gradually increase the tax on lots until all improvements and property are exempted from municipal taxation. . . . Prescott is nothing if not progressive.

Then, possibly due to Pauline's work for woman's suffrage, Buckey added, "In addition to this, all female tax-payers are accorded the right of suffrage on all municipal questions involving an election."

Henry George's ideas on the progressive rise of land values with the encroachment of civilization were echoed in Buckey's occasional letters to McClintock:

Thirty years ago the land on which it [Prescott] stands was bought for $200 and today it is rated at worth a million. This has been the rule all over the West. In no section of the world, perhaps, have land values—represented by city lots—increased so rapidly as in the western states of America during the last quarter of a century. Land bought at the government price of $1.25 an acre, in five, ten or fifteen years, has increased in many instances to millions.

After only a few months in office, Buckey managed also to stumble into a heated argument with the new governor, Myron Hawley McCord, a McKinley appointee who had taken office in Phoenix at about the time Buckey had become mayor of Prescott.

McCord, a Pennsylvania-born banker, newspaper publisher, and lumberman in Wisconsin, had served one undistinguished term in Congress before moving in 1893 to Arizona, where he had become part owner of the *Arizona Gazette* in Pheniz. During his term in Congress, McCord fortuitously had championed the candidacy of William McKinley for the House speakership against "Czar" Thomas B. Reed. In 1896 he had worked for McKinley's nomination at the St. Louis convention and as a reward for these services had received McKinley's nomination for the governorship.

McCord's confirmation ran into difficulty when it was widely rumored that his family had made a huge fortune in his congressional district as a result of land legislation he had authored. McCord's brother, moreover, had been prosecuted for fraud in connection with Indian lands in Wisconsin.

Buckey's run-in with the new governor had to do with a prison labor contract with the "State of Arizona Improvement Company," a corporation formed to dig a thirteen-mile-long irrigation canal above Yuma. Under terms of the extraordinary contract, the company would be supplied all the available prison labor it needed for ten years at seventy cents per man per day. These "wages" were to be paid by the corporation in "water rights," enabling the Territory to purchase water at regular rates to irrigate lands in the vicinity of the canal. The unusual contract further stipulated that the Territory was to bear all expenses for maintaining, transporting, and guarding the prisoners. There was no clause that limited use of the convict labor to the canal project. Eventually assigned to the canal construction were a hundred Yuma prisoners, who were credited with four days of prison time for each three days' work.

Buckey smelled a very big, very dead rat, just as had Mc-Cord's predecessor, Ben Franklin, who had assailed the contract vigorously and refused to recognize any part of it as legal. When McCord reinstated it, a number of prominent Arizonans attacked him in the Territory's various newspapers. One of the healthiest blasts, as might have been expected, came from Mayor O'Neill.

Buckey, in another of his famous "open letters," dated September 21, 1897, implied openly that McCord personally would benefit from the deceptive canal contract.

"The people of Arizona will never believe that you did it for nothing," he wrote.

They will not believe it because when you were a candidate for [appointment as] governor it was openly charged that if you were appointed you would be merely a tool to carry this contract into effect, a charge which you and your friends then emphatically denied. They will not believe it because of the dishonest manner in which you have sought to deceive them into believing that you were protecting their interest by modifying the contract, when in reality your acts have shown that you had no such intention.

Buckey's last paragraph left no question as to his own paid-in-full subscription to the rumors of McCord's cloudy business background:

. . . whether you were the rogue that some say in Wisconsin, or the fugitive timber thief of Arkansas lands, that, as others would have us believe, sought a haven from criminal prosecution in Arizona, does not enter into the controversy involving your official rectitude in the prison contract in Arizona.

The new governor had learned something about the new mayor of Prescott, the mayor had learned something about the governor, and neither was pleased.

Almost eleven years had passed since Buckey and Pauline's only child, "Buckey, Jr.," had died. Nothing could eradicate the memory of the few deliriously happy days they had experienced with the new son and nothing could erase the heartbreak of his death, or diminish their hope of having another child.

On October 13, 1897, Buckey and Pauline signed the papers to adopt a son. The boy, four years old, was named Morris, the son of Conrad O. and Maggie Piles. Legally adopted, Buckey's son became Morris—later Maurice—O'Neill.

It was only fitting that 1897, which began with the sadness of Captain John O'Neill's death, should end in such happiness.

CHAPTER TWENTY

Remember the Maine!

THE MORE FARSIGHTED of Prescott's residents —especially seasoned army men at Whipple Barracks—felt a war with Spain inevitable long before the U.S. battleship *Maine* had set out ominously to make a "courtesy call" at Havana, Cuba. Some had foreseen eventual involvement in Cuba as far back as the beginning of 1896, when insurgents on the island had succeeded in harassing Spanish troops to the extent that Spain dispatched its foremost soldier, Valeriano Weyler y Nicolau, to quell the uprising. Most people, however, were simply ardent newspaper readers and were not privy to military sensibilities and foresight. But they did, as they would recall later, begin having more than a passing interest in the Cuban situation about the time the imperious Captain-General Weyler stepped ashore at Havana.

No man of his time was to be so execrated as Captain-General Weyler. Newspapers called him "the most bloodthirsty general in the world," and his ferocity was compared with that of the Turkish bashi-bazouks who had spitted babies on bayonets, tortured and mutilated, burned, and raped their way across Bulgaria just twenty years earlier. Weyler was nicknamed "Butcher," and it stuck. American newspapers, some of which had kept correspondents in Cuba since the beginning of the rebellion against Spanish control in 1895, followed and damned Weyler's every move. Leading the field of denunciators were the *New York Journal*, under the awesomely yellow leadership of William Randolph Hearst, and the *New York World*, a great newspaper trembling on the brink of Hearstmanship, led by Joseph Pulitzer. They were the chief makers of devils among the Spaniards and elevators to sainthood of such native insur-

gent leaders as Máximo Gómez and Calixto García, to whom
a famous message soon would be delivered and the act im-
mortalized by Elbert Hubbard.

By the fall of 1896, Weyler had succeeded in implementing
a hard-nosed program aimed at breaking up the supply lines of
the *insurrectos*. The word for this program became known to
newspaper readers everywhere, few of whom could pronounce
or spell it—*reconcentrado*. It meant simply that Weyler had
ordered the rural Cuban populace concentrated in villages and
towns to prevent them from sending food and other supplies
out into the countryside. The effect of this innovation was to
rob the insurgents—used to posing as simple peasants and
farmers—of food and supplies. This move, coupled with
Weyler's constant pressure on guerrilla bands roaming the
provinces, succeeded spectacularly but brought on several side
effects that boded ill for his chances of victory. Food became
scarce everywhere, and the innocent as well as the guilty suffered from famine and disease. Moreover, Weyler's merciless-
ness (not to mention his distaste and well-placed distrust in
American newspapermen) brought the extremest calumny
down on his head in America—a smoldering fire fanned and
fed by a hugely successful Cuban-junta propaganda machine
in New York.

Spain, suffering from complicated and perverse longings—to
suppress the Cuban uprising, to avoid war with America—
eventually recalled Weyler, but the coals were hot and this
splash of water only seemed to put them out.

President Cleveland withstood all the press clamor, stoutly
proclaiming neutrality and politely asking the Spanish government if it could not end hostilities on the island. He informed
the Spaniards that he could not speak for the incoming administration's attitudes toward intervention.

Kindly William McKinley tried his best to follow in Cleveland's footsteps. He did not want war and told the Spanish
pointedly he thought the *reconcentrado* system ought to be

brought to an end and some peaceful solution—perhaps a revision of Spain's colonial policy on the island—inaugurated. Though it obviously raked against his grain, McKinley did warn Spain that the United States might be forced to intervene unless the situation perceptibly and quickly cooled.

In the summer of 1897, not long after Buckey had been elected mayor of Prescott, he read in both the *Miner* and the *Courier* the news of the assassination of Spanish premier Cánovas by an Italian anarchist. Cánovas' replacement was Práxedes Mateo Sagasta, who appeared to be capable of turning the tide of war that had been washing America's shore. By the end of the year, at least a token autonomy had been granted to the Cubans, and Captain-General Weyler was recalled and replaced by a kindlier, or at least less noticeable, man. Things were looking up—momentarily.

The brittle façade of peace and new programs quickly began to disintegrate toward the end of 1897, when insurgent mobs rioted and stormed up and down the streets of Havana. The most serious mistake in this development, as it turned out, was that the Cubans actually were threatening American life and property this time, not just their own. And for just such a contingency, the *Maine* had been detached from the North Atlantic squadron on October 8, and her captain, Charles D. Sigsbee, ordered to take her to Port Royal, South Carolina.

Two months later, the *Maine* proceeded to Key West, jumping-off place for Cuba, just ninety-odd miles south, and Captain Sigsbee had been notified that if he received the code words "Two Dollars" from the U.S. Consul in Havana, Fitzhugh Lee, the *Maine* was to repair posthaste to the Cuban capital.

Late in January, 1898, Navy Secretary John Long effected a "friendly" visit to Havana for the *Maine*. In arranging this "courtesy call," Long may have had the help of his assistant, Theodore Roosevelt, whom he sometimes found exasperating, though helpful and loyal. Although some in the press labeled the visit a "gun-boat calling card," Captain Sigsbee was able to drop anchor in Havana Harbor on January 25 for three weeks of uninterrupted, if watchful, Spanish cordiality.

At nine-forty on the night of February 15, all that ended. The *Maine* rode snugly at anchor; boatswains had screeched "pipe down," and Captain Sigsbee sat in his cabin writing a letter to his wife. Taps had sounded at nine-ten and, while the carnival season in the city had poured hundreds of celebrants into the streets, not a sound interrupted the tranquility of the *Maine*.

At 20 minutes before 10, the *Maine* shuddered and racked with an ear-splitting explosion that shattered window glass in the city and sent rocket-like fingers of brilliant light hurtling skyward from the ship's mangled decks, casting a brief reflection on the water like roman candles. In seconds the *Maine* became a crushed mass of floating wreckage, listing, rumbling, scraping metal on metal, and settling in 30 feet of water, convulsed by internal explosions as flames leaped from one ammunition locker to another. In a few more minutes the great ship had heeled ignominiously and sunk, with only her superstructure poking above the lapping water. She took 263 men to their deaths.

Captain Sigsbee, last to leave the ship, climbed into his gig and made his way to the *City of Washington*, an American steamer nearby. Sigsbee walked among the wounded men gathered on the decks of the *Washington* and watched briefly from the rail as the *Maine* continued to shudder with fitful, convulsive explosions. The captain then wrote his message to Washington, informing Secretary Long of the tragedy and making the futile observation, "Public opinion should be suspended until further report."

But it was too late for that. The gun was cocked and a finger lay on the hair trigger.

Pauline O'Neill, in later years, would remember her husband's reaction to the news of the *Maine* sinking. The *New York*

Journal plainly said it had resulted from a mine, torpedo, or other "infernal machine," and openly speculated on "Spanish responsibility," "Sigsbee's suspicions," and the reports of one man who claimed to have heard the entire plot to blow up the ship.

"When the Maine was blown up," Pauline wrote, "and the whole nation was discussing the question of the war that might follow, Mr. O'Neill felt that his country would demand his services. A meeting was held here [in Prescott] in the courthouse on the evening following the receipt of the news. Mr. O'Neill again declared that he was ready and willing to shed his heart's last drop for his flag, his country."

A few days after the courthouse meeting, in which Mayor O'Neill and virtually every able-bodied man in town hotly discussed the onrushing war, two Cuban junta officers touring the West to plead the cause of "Cuba Libre" lectured at the Yavapai Courthouse. The junta representatives craftily emphasized the long history of Spanish abuse in Cuba's struggle, which they compared with the American war for independence. Buckey presided over the lecture and introduced the Cuban officers. When the speeches ended, the crowd pledged a substantial sum of money to the insurgents' war coffers and passed a resolution asking Congress to recognize the junta and furnish assistance.

All during February, March, and early April, plans were being drawn up in Prescott to insure some participation in what promised to be the first war in thirty-three years. Everybody knew the war was coming; it was no longer a military vision, but a matter of time. No one believed it could be far off.

Buckey practically suspended all city business but the most necessary and routine to bend his mind to the task of preparing for the coming conflict. His two closest confidants in the planning were Jim McClintock, the Phoenix newspaperman whom Buckey had known ever since coming to Arizona in 1879, and Alexander O. Brodie, 1870 West Point graduate, Indian fighter, engineer, cattleman, and miner whom Buckey had met during the Walnut Creek disaster. Another whom Buckey invited to listen was his younger brother, Eugene Brady O'Neill, who had returned to Arizona with Buckey after their father's death and who now was practicing law in Phoenix.

With the approval of Governor McCord, who rather graciously suspended his dislike of Buckey and the Prescott mayor's too-ready tongue and pen, McClintock, Brodie, and Mayor O'Neill began putting together a plan for Arizona's contribution to the war effort, if and when the declaration came.

The plan called for making up a full regiment of volunteer cavalry, consisting of 3 squadrons of 4 troops each, a total of 1,056 men. Each troop, led by one captain and two lieutenants, would have 85 enlisted men. Buckey and Jim McClintock were to recruit 6 troops each; Brodie was to be the regimental colonel.

This plan, McClintock would always maintain, was Buckey's idea from the start. McClintock said that he and Buckey approached Brodie with the idea and sold the former Indian fighter on it. The historian of the Arizona volunteers of 1898, Charles Herner, believes most, if not all, of the planning derived from Brodie and finds support in contemporary newspaper accounts. But the point is moot. Buckey O'Neill, if not author of the plan, became its main force, life blood, most energetic champion, and soon its principal hero.

Brodie, whatever his role in developing the idea, quickly took the role of old soldier. On March 3, he shot off telegrams to President McKinley and Governor McCord offering his services in the event of war and requesting permission to raise a volunteer cavalry regiment in Arizona Territory. On March 10, in a letter to the president, he renewed his requests. On April 2, Governor McCord also asked McKinley to appoint Brodie to collect his Arizona volunteers, assuring the president that "no better material for cavalry purposes can be found anywhere in the world, than among the cowboys of Arizona."

On March 13, the letter-writing campaign in full swing, Buckey wrote McClintock:

It looks now as if war is sure to come. The President's message on Tuesday will pave the way for it. Of course, it will not be declared then. Time sufficient to let our government put crews on newly purchased ships and get them out beyond the league line will be sparred for, by making some demand on Spain that that country cannot fulfill, and which demand will in itself be tantamount to a declaration of hostilities. I think this is the course that McKinley will adopt in order to force Spain's hands. In my opinion there is not doubt but that he wants war, and has wanted it for the last six months. It means everything to him in the way of a re-election.

Except for the idea that McKinley wanted war, the letter honestly appraised the growing war hysteria of the country. In the ensuing weeks, the president would attempt to settle the crisis through diplomatic channels, asking the Spanish government to call an armistice on the island and to grant Cuba "full self-government." And Spain, certainly dreading a war she knew herself woefully ill-prepared to fight (but unaware of America's comparable predicament), was willing to do anything short of extending full independence.

But that, plainly enough, was not a sufficient concession.

CHAPTER TWENTY-ONE

The Cowboy Regiment

MARCH ENDED with the findings of the *Maine* court of inquiry, which was convened in Havana and headed by the respected Rear Admiral William T. Sampson. The court grimly and meticulously had examined the wreckage of the fatal ship, questioned witnesses, crewmen, and Captain Sigsbee, and issued its report to Congress on March 28. The court concluded that a submarine mine had caused the detonation of at least two of the forward magazines of the ship. The court of inquiry report was prim and matter-of-fact, but that made no difference. The American newspaper-reading public had been primed for the findings: any external explosion should be synonymous with Spanish guilt, and of course the "submarine mine" was an external device; it was as simple as that.

The attitude prevailed at the beginning of April that the hour at last had arrived. It found a home in high circles, too, and Under Secretary of the Navy Theodore Roosevelt quickly announced his intention of resigning his post to take part in the coming conflict. McKinley's Secretary of War, Russell Alger, even offered a colonelcy of volunteers but Roosevelt, in a remarkable attack of self-restraint, wisely demurred in favor of his friend Leonard Wood, who was President and Mrs. McKinley's physician.

Roosevelt accomplished one signal act before his departure from Long's department. During the absence of the secretary, ten days after the *Maine* disaster, Roosevelt cabled orders to Commodore George Dewey of the Asiatic Squadron to mobilize his ships at Hong Kong, to keep them fully coaled, and, in the event of a declaration of war, to proceed to the Philippine Archipelago for "offensive operations." Long did not rescind the order on his return to Washington, and Dewey scurried to paint his white ships gray. He purchased a collier full of coal, had his vessels' bottoms scraped and hulls repaired, and provisioned the fleet for whatever exigency might arise.

In Yavapai and Maricopa counties, meantime, preparations began taking on more realistic aspects—the recruiting of volunteers that hopefully would be welded into an entire regiment of Arizonans.

On the paperwork side, Governor McCord kept busy with correspondence with the president. McCord had a genius for amassing sensible evidence in support of his drive to have the Arizona regiment accepted for service in unmutilated form— the way Arizona wanted it, not necessarily the way the War Department wanted it. McCord dispatched to his benefactor, President McKinley, a barrage of letters asserting with conviction and logic that his territorials would require little training since they already were skilled in horsemanship and firearms and were familiar with camp equipment; that they would have no fear of hostile gunfire, since many had campaigned against the Apache; that they would be well suited for outpost duty because of their natural self-reliance and knowledge of the Spanish language; and that, coming from the Southwest, they would have a natural tolerance for semi-tropical climes that could not be found in men from colder regions.

Alex Brodie, at the same time, checked with Buckey and Jim McClintock on recruiting progress, and learned that about half the requisite number of men had pledged enlistment. Buckey, working the northern part of the Territory, wrote to McClintock, in the south, that he would furnish men to McClintock if the southern Territorials failed to respond in adequate numbers. There appeared to Buckey to be an unsatisfactory response to the call for pledged enlistments but he knew, if the war declaration came, he would be turning men away.

During the second week of April, President McKinley had

pinned his hopes for avoiding armed intervention in Cuba on diplomatic negotiations, including entreaties from the pope to Spain's queen regent. Although, on April 9, the queen had instructed the suspension of armed hostilities in Cuba, the armistice declaration was too late. McKinley, through his efforts to avoid war, had called down the wrath of his own party against him. Resolutions by Congress and ultimatums framed by the State Department resulted in Spain's severing diplomatic relations with the United States on April 21. The day before, Congress had authorized President McKinley to use military force to secure the independence of Cuba and end the internecine conflict there.

Every passing day marked a sort of turning point. On April 22, the great news to Buckey, Brodie, McClintock, and McCord was the introduction of a volunteer bill authorizing the raising of a regiment of volunteers from the Western states and territories. When the bill was amended, it read, "The Secretary of War [is authorized] to organize companies, troops, battalions or regiments, not to exceed 3,000 men" from the West. The amendment permitted the formation of *three* full cavalry regiments from the states and territories of the West.

Then on April 25 came two more crucial developments: war was officially declared against Spain, and Secretary Alger dispatched to Governor McCord a message that proved to be the keystone and the genesis of the troops soon to become known as the "Rough Riders." Alger wrote: "The President directs that Capt. Leonard Wood of the U.S. Army be authorized to raise a regiment of cowboys and mounted riflemen, and to be its Colonel, and has named Hon. Theodore Roosevelt as Lt. Colonel. All other officers will come from the vicinity where the troops are raised. What can you do for them?"

McCord, of course, could do plenty, once he managed to hide his great disappointment. Clearly, Arizona would not be supplying a full regiment for the war effort. In fact, as the details emerged, only 170 men were needed from the entire Territory. A long step backward from the 1,000-man regiment originally envisioned. Colonel Wood's First U.S. Volunteer Cavalry Regiment was to be organized in all 4 territories— Arizona and Indian Territory (the eastern part of the present state of Oklahoma) would supply 170 men each; New Mexico, 340; Oklahoma, 80. There was nothing to do but swallow this bitter pill. McCord did receive permission from Secretary Alger to name the senior regimental major, and without hesitation he selected Alex Brodie.

Brodie threw himself into his task, forwarding to the governor his choices for the two troop captains for the Arizona unit —William O. O'Neill of Prescott and James McClintock of Phoenix. McCord approved McClintock unhesitatingly but lingered a bit over Buckey's name. The governor still bore scorch marks from the Prescott mayor's blistering letters on the prison-labor contract and, like all seasoned politicians, he hesitated to reward political enemies. McClintock, Brodie, and several other influentials visited McCord personally over the O'Neill appointment, and the governor finally relented.

One of Buckey's friends is said to have argued with McCord, perhaps facetiously, perhaps not, that Buckey would not be embarrassing the governor with newspaper articles and letters while off dodging bullets in the Cuban jungles.

Two days after the war declaration, Arizona recruiters began conducting their duties in makeshift offices set up in the Aitken and Robinson Cigar Store in downtown Prescott. Buckey, McClintock, and Brodie personally interviewed the prospects in the Yavapai County Courthouse. The mayor worked busily behind his desk, puffing an endless series of roll-your-owns and bumming matches from McClintock or anyone else handy. The main criteria for enlistment were that the applicants be eighteen to forty-five, physically sound, good horsemen, and good shots.

Those recruits passing the gauntlet of interviewers and medicos were marched the three miles to Whipple Barracks and assigned a bunk, given a blanket and mess equipment, and told to wait. Whipple Barracks, established in 1864 northeast of

Prescott, had been an important frontier army post. As Fort Whipple in 1870, it had been the home of the Military Department of Arizona. Since 1879, it had borne the name Whipple Barracks. But despite its illustrious history, the recruits found the place cold, their bunks hard as a rock and acrawl with vermin. Furthermore, the army rations of coffee, bacon, beans, hash, beef, soup, and hardtack were monotonous and tasteless. As a result, Prescott's restaurants and Whiskey Row establishments did a land-office business. During the hot afternoons and chilly evenings, the volunteers crowded into the Row and visited as many establishments as they could before running shy of money. "The Palace," run by Robert Brow, seemed a particular favorite, and Brow resolved to do something for the men to express his appreciation for their patronage.

Major Brodie, as the recruiting proceeded toward the end of April, received notice from the War Department that the First U.S. Volunteer Cavalry Regiment's complement had been increased to 1,000 men, raising Arizona's quota from 170 to 200 men. The War Department order represented only a slight improvement over the original disappointment, but the three volunteer officers were far too busy with their recruiting and organizing duties to anguish long.

Another pressing problem had to do with assignment of subordinate officers for the troops under Buckey's and McClintock's captaincies. McClintock chose for first lieutenant Joseph L. B. Alexander, a forty-year-old Phoenix lawyer; as second lieutenant, George B. Wilcox of Bisbee, an enlisted veteran of the Fourth U.S. Cavalry.

Three men applied for commissions as first lieutenant in Captain O'Neill's troop, one of them being Buckey's younger brother Eugene, barely a year in the Territory. Eugene had been admitted to the bar in Washington in 1889 and practiced law in his home town before joining Buckey in Arizona after the death of their father. The other applicants were Kean St. Charles of Kingman and Frank Frantz, an Illinoisian who had served as a mining company clerk near Prescott. Although it is not known precisely how the selection was made, Buckey could not be accused of nepotism; Frantz won the post as first lieutenant, and Robert S. Patterson of Safford was chosen as second lieutenant.

On April 27, Buckey traveled to Phoenix to receive his captain's bars from the governor. Pauline later recalled:

Until he received his commission, I would not believe that he was in earnest. He laughed and joked about going, and I thought that the idea that he was needed had left him. On the 28th of April he returned from Phoenix with the captaincy in his pocket, and the following day he was mustered in—the first volunteer in the whole United States to offer his services.

Volunteer Number One, Mayor William O. O'Neill of Prescott, did indeed swell with pride over his distinction. April 30 had been set as the formal enrollment date for the volunteers and their officers but Buckey, maintaining his lifelong propensity for frenetic enthusiasm for anything resembling a *cause*, took the oath the day before and secured the honor to which Pauline—with no little pride herself—alluded.

CHAPTER TWENTY-TWO

Off to War for the Bould Sojer Boys

ALEX BRODIE RECEIVED a telegram from Colonel Leonard Wood on May 1, instructing that the Arizona recruits be brought on to San Antonio, and on May 4 the Arizonans were gathered in Prescott for the leave-taking.

The departure called for an impressive ceremony, the likes of which Prescott had never before witnessed, and city fathers —particularly Mayor O'Neill's council members—determined to bring it off with class. At four in the hot and wet afternoon, led by the blare of the Prescott Brass Band, the volunteers lined up, nondescript, to say the least, in their unmilitary variety of dress. Down the line of recruits one could see stetsons, straw boaters, and floppy fedoras; rumpled suit coats with unmatching trousers; vests, stiff celluloid collars, starched collars, open collars, no collars; string ties, black bunched-up ties, no ties; boots worn out, new boots, and low-heeled shoes. The owners of such attire carried battered grips, bedrolls, cardboard suitcases, bags, and valises.

The procession of volunteers, officers, and bandsmen marched out of step to the grounds in front of the courthouse and formed in zig-zagging ranks on the north side of the plaza to listen to an address by Governor McCord, who had come from Phoenix that morning to participate, doubtless wondering, too, of his own future in the war.

The governor brought with him a regimental flag, hand-sewn in silk by the Women's Relief Corps of Phoenix, an affiliate of the local GAR chapter. Presenting the silk banner to Major Brodie, McCord charged each volunteer to keep his promise that the flag "would be carried by his battalion to the front and would be found, like the plume of Henry of Navarre, waving in the fore-front of battle."

R. Allyn Lewis, the territorial adjutant general, presented the officer's commissions; Reese M. Ling, Prescott's city attorney, introduced Mayor O'Neill and called him to the bandstand to present him with an engraved six-shooter and tooled holster. Each trooper then was given a colored hatband to identify his unit: red for Buckey's Troop A, blue for McClintock's B Troop. The A Troopers' red bands led McClintock's men to refer to them as "The Salvation Army Gang," and "Buckey's boys," not to be outdone, tagged McClintock's men as "Band of Hope Boys."

Prescott saloonkeeper Bob Brow, fulfilling his vow to do something for the "boys," came up with a mascot for the troopers, a feisty mountain lion named Florence.

The ceremonies ended, the raw troopers marched down Montezuma Street, accompanied by Governor McCord and his staff, the Prescott Brass Band, Civil War veterans, the Volunteer Fire Department, and a swarm of gay school children to whom a parade of any kind meant a lark. At the end of the march, the five waiting railroad cars were decorated with bunting, streamers, and slogans such as "The Arizona Cowboy Regiment" and "Remember the *Maine!*" The cars had been equipped with generous stocks of boiled ham, mutton, pig's feet, canned fruit, bread, pickles, and three barrels filled with iced bottled beer. Three hundred corncob pipes also had been donated by some knowledgeable well-wisher.

With the choir from the Territorial Normal School singing "God Be With You Till We Meet Again," the 210 recruits and their officers clambered aboard the train, a special of the Santa Fe, Prescott, and Phoenix Railroad consisting of 4 passenger cars and a combination car. At 7:15 P.M., it pulled out of the station amidst a sea of waving handkerchiefs, old timers' salutes, flag-waving, and raucous cheers.

Captain McClintock said later, "It should be told that when

the Arizona contingent of the regiment was being raised, there was no knowledge of its ultimate destination in a military sense." And this held true even to the moment of boarding the train. The volunteers knew only that they were heading for San Antonio, Texas, gathering place for the First U.S. Volunteer Cavalry Regiment, and that they were going by way of Albuquerque and, after changing to a Southern Pacific train, El Paso, and thence to the Alamo City. After that it was anybody's guess but most hoped they would get to Cuba, or wherever the fighting was taking place, before the fighting stopped.

A few days before leaving, Buckey and a Prescott friend, P. C. Bicknell, had visited the Grand Canyon. Bicknell recalled that the two of them "wandered out on the commanding promontory, east of where the Bright Angel Hotel now stands, and watched the sunset." Bicknell said Buckey spoke of the war only briefly but dwelled lovingly on the wonders of the canyon and pointed out one particular butte that was painted in lavender and gold by the sunset. Buckey remarked that it reminded him of Kipling's "Old Moulmein Pagoda."

On the evening of April 27, Buckey and Pauline had gone down to Phoenix, where the officers of the Arizona volunteers were being honored at a special banquet. The adjutant general, R. Allyn Lewis, proposed a toast to the assembled officers: "Now we drink the soldier's toast—death or a star!" Buckey jumped to his feet and, holding high his glass, responded, "Who would not gamble for a new star?"

To some, Buckey's meaning was clear; to others it indicated that the Prescott mayor hoped to return home at least a brigadier general.

Pauline's recollections of Buckey's final departure had a poignant note: "I went to the train on May 4 to see the gallant men leave," she recalled. "My eyes were tearless, while my heart was wrung in agony. At the last goodbye he said: 'My dear, the war will not last long, and I will return in ninety days.' But my heart kept repeating, 'Forever, Forever!'"

Later Pauline must have thought of a story Buckey had

written four days earlier, "A Day's Round Up." In it an Irishman named Kelly sang a ditty with a refrain that was painfully appropriate for Buckey O'Neill's new profession:

> Oh, there's not a thrade that's going,
> Worth following or worth knowing,
> Like that from glory growing,
> For a bould sojer boy.

The journey to Flagstaff turned out to be a highlight of the entire trip. A rousing demonstration of townspeople met the train, and morale could not have been higher if the troopers were coming home from the war instead of going off to it. Albuquerque and El Paso were exceedingly hot but, again, such discomforts were offset by the heroic efforts of the towns along the route to show their unqualified pride and support by pouring into the depots to shout congratulations, pump hands, slap backs, cheer, and wave flags. Thus, even the long haul across Texas was not wholly miserable, although the cramped coaches, filled with long and lean men jackknifed into uncomfortable proximity, tended to bring out tempers, even among comrades about to be in arms.

All during the sweaty train ride, Buckey and Tom Rynning, —McClintock's crusty top sergeant with *regular army* (magic phrase) experience—kept up a running battle to get rations to their troopers first. At each chow stop, Buckey maneuvered his men to the doors and led them into the nearest diner or restaurant while Rynning's charges were still unfolding from their coach seats. But Rynning got his chance to even the score when the train steamed into Del Rio, Texas, just across the Rio Grande from the mud buildings of Villa Acuña, Mexico. Rynning's version of the story follows:

I had the edge on Buckey one way. I'd been over that line before and he hadn't. So pulling into Del Rio, I says just loud enough for him to overhear me, "Get ready, you mavericks, to beat these other dogies to the feed trough. The eating-house is right on the south side of the tracks."

It wasn't though. It was north of the railroad. I'd coached my bunch on the quiet, and as the train began to slack up we was all crowding the south steps, and Buckey and his hostiles crowded right down there with us. Then as they all piled off just as the train stopped, we rushed across the platforms to the north side and had all the seats in the dining room taken when Buckey had give up trying to find any eats on the south side of the track, and he had to stand around cussing me till we got outside our chow.

Just before dawn on May 7, the S. P. ground to a halt, spurting jets of steam, at the San Antonio station. The Arizonans, stiff and sweaty from the boring sixty-hour haul from Prescott, found to their delight that they were the first volunteer contingent to arrive. At the Southern Pacific station, Captains O'Neill and McClintock joined Major Brodie in gathering the men for the streetcar ride out to the fairground at Riverside Park, three miles south of the city on the San Antonio River, selected as their training ground.

The Edison Car Line discharged its passengers at "Camp Wood," the former fairgrounds, and the volunteers were marched to their billets, the floor of the barn-like two-story Exposition Building with its ornate cupola, where they stowed their belongings, ate a hot breakfast and, later in the morning, visited the town, saw the sights, and soaked up a moderate portion of the nickel beer being sold at bars and stands around the camp.

The next day, Buckey, Brodie, McClintock, and the other officers of the Arizona contingent, met formally with their commanding officer, Leonard Wood.

Wood already had compiled an extraordinary army record. Born in Winchester, New Hampshire, in the same year as Buckey—1860—he had graduated from Harvard Medical School in 1884. After a brief period in private practice, he had gone to Arizona as a contract surgeon with the Fourth U.S. Cavalry. Plunging into the Apache compaign, he had won a Medal of Honor for a May, 1885, exploit, carrying dispatches on a one-hundred-mile horseback journey through countryside teeming with hostiles. In 1891, Wood had been promoted to a captaincy and four years later received the "plum" assignment as physician to President and Mrs. McKinley, the latter long ailing and requiring constant medical attention.

Among the many friends Wood gathered during his tour of duty in the capital, one of his closest was Under Secretary of Navy Theodore Roosevelt. The friendship worked both ways, and Roosevelt had recommended the Indian fighter-physician to War Secretary Alger as the best man to command the First Volunteer Cavalry. Roosevelt, yet to arrive in the San Antonio encampment, became Alger's choice to serve as Wood's second in command.

Wood's many attributes included intelligence, sensitivity, fairness, and a proper, though not overbearing, military dignity. All this earned him the unqualified respect of those who served with him. For Wood—cool, quiet, undemonstrative, and military—the key word among his troopers and officers was *respect*. For Roosevelt—unmilitary, bearish, loquacious, glad-handing, and exuberant—the word was *adoration*.

In retrospect, it seems strange that two men with such diverse personalities could make any kind of efficient command out of the raw materials gathered for their regiment. But, so far as is known, Wood and Roosevelt had no serious falling out; indeed, they complemented each other and came close at times to working miracles as a command team.

The Riverside Park encampment was ringed picturesquely with hackberry, pecan, cottonwood, and sycamore trees. Wood, with the Arizona officers and Major George Dunn—a Denver native, later to command the regiment's third squadron—inspected the site and expressed satisfaction with the facilities. The Colonel instructed that officers' tents should be erected between the main entrance to the camp and the enlisted men's billet, but issued no other immediate orders until the remaining recruits arrived.

Camp Wood was in readiness for the Rough Riders.

CHAPTER TWENTY-THREE

The Rough Riders

DURING THE FIRST 2 weeks of May the other volunteers who would join the Arizonans to make up the First U.S. Volunteer Cavalry Regiment began drifting into Camp Wood: the Oklahoma contingent, the 340 men from New Mexico Territory, the 170 from Indian Territory.[8] Too, the raising of the regimental quota from 780 to 1,000 men permitted the commingling with the Westerners of an assortment of "Easterners," organized by Roosevelt's friend Guy Murchie of Harvard University.

On May 9, the first of these "society swells," "dudes," and "la-de-dah boys," as the crusty territorial cowboys, prospectors, hunters, and range riders variously called them, began showing up at the camp—some with expensive luggage, strange sounding names, and clipped accents, and a few with built-in sneers. They were scattered into several troops, but one group formed their own special unit (Troop K), and thus managed to stick together, establishing their headquarters in the east end of Exposition Hall.

With the mixing of the "dudes" into the regiment, the Rough Riders—a name already gaining currency in San Antonio newspapers—came to epitomize Theodore Roosevelt's own twin strains of hero worship. The eastern seaboard "swells" represented the Rooseveltian aristocrat: athletic, collegiate, Boston, Harvard, Princeton, Yale. These included, among those Roose-

---

[8] Indian Territory was the name commonly applied to the eastern part of Oklahoma, into which the Five Civilized Tribes—Cherokee, Creek, Seminole, Choctaw, and Chickasaw—were removed from 1820 to 1845. Other tribes followed. The Indian Territory, never formally organized, demised in 1907 with the admission of Oklahoma as a state.

velt liked best to single out, Dudley Dean, Harvard quarterback; Bob Wrenn, also quarterback and tennis star; Waller, the high jumper; Horace Devereaux, Harvard football great; Craig Wadsworth, steeplechase rider; Hamilton Fish, excaptain of the Columbia crew; Woodbury Kane, cousin of John Jacob Astor and Harvard yachtsman; and members of Roosevelt's Oyster Bay polo team, Elliott Cowdin, Harry Thorpe, and Munro Furguson.

In ultimate contrast stood the Westerners—"Tall and sinewy," Roosevelt described them, "with resolute, weather-beaten faces and eyes that looked a man straight in the face without flinching . . . to a man born adventurers, in the old sense of the word."

Mostly, these adventurers were cowboys, prospectors, a few drifters, and ne'er-do-wells, hunters of game—and an occasional manhunter. Some of them had seen service on both sides of the bars, such as tough old notch-eared Benjamin Franklin Daniels, one-time marshal of Dodge City, Kansas; Guthrie, Oklahoma; and Cripple Creek, Colorado. Other notables included Sherman Bell, deputy marshal of Cripple Creek; Crockett, a Georgian who had been, among several occupations, a "revenooer," and had waged war against moonshiners in several locales; and Fred Herrig, a northern Idaho hunter-trapper who had led Roosevelt on hunting expeditions into the most obscure backwaters of the Northwest.

Some of the lean and sunbaked Westerners were known by nickname only: "Cherokee Bill," "Happy Jack," "Smokey Moore," "Rattlesnake Pete," "Tough Ike," "Prayerful James" (one of the most sulfurous and inventive cussers in the regiment), "Metropolitan Bill," "The Dude," and "Sheeny Solomon," the latter a red-haired Irishman. A favorite among the cowboys was "Little Billy" McGinty, a wiry Oklahoma wrangler and bronc buster. Among the many stories that circulated about McGinty, a favorite concerned his absolute and unwavering inability to stay in step on the parade ground. After repeated chewings-out, the hangdog Little Billy finally im-

plored, "Let me git my pony. I'm purty sure I kin keep in step
on horseback!"

"In all the world," Roosevelt wrote, "there could be no better
material for soldiers than that afforded by these grim hunters
of the mountains, these wild rough riders of the plains."

Of all of them, Roosevelt repeatedly chose Buckey O'Neill
for special praise:

> . . . he was himself a born soldier, a born leader of men. He was a
> wild, reckless fellow, soft-spoken, and of dauntless courage and bound-
> less ambition; he was stanchly loyal to his friends and cared for his
> men in every way.

Roosevelt's judgment won a quick second from Sergeant
Harbo "Tom" Rynning, who recalled that, during the San
Antonio interlude, when Captain O'Neill served as officer of
the day, "I sat up late with him, teaching him how to go
through the routine of regimental guard-mount. He was very
intelligent and learned quickly." After Rynning's coaching,
based on his regular cavalry experiences in the Indian campaigns, "Buckey, as officer of the day, went through guard-
mount like a veteran," Rynning said, "a natural-born soldier."

The San Antonio newspapers speculated, hopefully one sus-
pects, that the Eastern dudes and Western cowpokes would
clash sooner or later. A few days before Roosevelt arrived in
camp, the *Express* reported:

> The Texas cowboys who have the pleasure to mess with this party
> of New York "high rollers" will have an enjoyable time, so long as
> they are in camp in San Antonio. Ninety percent of them carry a
> large wad in their side pockets with which to play a little game of
> draw and large bank accounts behind them. Some of them have their
> "men" with them to care for their uniforms and top boots at a salary
> of $60 a month, also to cook at $100 a month.

There were few valets and cooks, actually, but the enlisted
trooper, receiving thirteen dollars a month in pay, no doubt
thought there were far too many.

Still, few physical confrontations occurred among the Rough
Riders themselves and between the troopers and San Antonians.

Captain O'Neill, commanding Troop A, First U.S. Volunteer Cavalry Regiment. Taken in San Antonio, 1898.

Officers' Mess, Rough Rider encampment at San Antonio, 1898. At the head of

Cowboys and Oyster Bay polo players blended together in the humid Texas summer heat, dressed in slouch hats, khaki uniforms, leggings, and dust-begrimed boots, handkerchiefs knotted loosely about their necks, cowboy style. All dug ditches, built fires for the cooks, and carried forage for their animals.

One natural-born gripe, the *one* in the phrase "There's one in every outfit," was William Tiffany, nephew of Mrs. August Belmont, who complained of the lack of hot water for bathing, the food—which he described as "nauseating"—and of the publicity that seemed to follow the Rough Riders, particularly after the arrival of Theodore Roosevelt. But the Tiffanys constituted a minority. There was a distinct flavor of informality among the volunteers—most of them simple men who didn't know a smart salute from a bag of Bull Durham. Roosevelt later savored one story that illustrated this humorous, sometimes (to the regular army noncoms) exasperating, nonregulation behavior.

On a particularly hot night in San Antonio, Roosevelt and Wood returned to their tents to escape the swarms of mosquitos that infested the camp. Between their command tents they found a sentry, one of the Western boys, who had thrown his rifle to the ground and was vigorously slapping the mosquitos that had crawled beneath his shirt and trouser legs. Noting the two officers staring, the sentry nodded pleasantly, barely missing a slap, and said with a grimace, "Ain't they bad?"

The month at Riverside Park settled into a routine. Reveille sounded at five-thirty, followed by stables, breakfast, mounting of the guard, drill—endless drill—the noon chow, more afternoon drill, mail call at four, retreat at six, supper, tattoo at eight-thirty, taps at nine.

Colonel Wood attended to the ordnance for his regiment by ceaseless pressure and, with Roosevelt's considerable arm-bending and cumshawing in Washington, was able to secure Krag-Jorgensen rifles for the entire regiment. This was a 6-shot, bolt-action, .30-caliber piece using smokeless powder and rated an excellent weapon. Those regulars not fortunate enough to get one had to make do with the old 1873 model Springfield .45-.70, which still used black powder. McClellan saddles became standard equipment for the regiment but gained little popularity with the cowboys accustomed to the large and comfortable stock saddle. And, instead of cavalry sabers, officers and enlisted men were issued machetes and a "cavalry style" .45 pistol. Each issue also included holster, cartridge belt, bridle, water bridle, halter, saddlebags, surcingle, picket pin and rope, nosebag, currycomb, brush, spurs, canteen, mess pan, tin cup, poncho, body blanket, horse blanket, half a shelter tent, and a service belt.

The regiment's pack train arrived from St. Louis not long after the troopers had settled into their routine. Each troop tried to select a different horse color to distinguish itself from the others: Buckey's A Troop took bays, McClintock's B Troopers sorrels; others took roans, browns, grays, or whatever was left.

By the time Roosevelt arrived on May 15, the Southern Pacific depot had been decorated with an enormous sign proclaiming "THIS WAY TO ROOSEVELT'S ROUGH RIDER CAMP," which some thought would embarrass Colonel Wood but which did not. Roosevelt's arrival at half past seven that morning, however, did signal to many that the regiment at last was getting girded up to go somewhere besides to the drill field or the nickel-beer saloon. The lieutenant colonel hopped off the S. P. coach in time to hear, above hissing jets of steam, the welcoming tunes of San Antonio's famous German bandmaster, "Professor" Carl Beck. Roosevelt was dressed in a uniform of tan duck material, the trousers stuffed into spit-polished cordovan boots. The stand-up collar of his khaki jacket bore the bold initials "U.S.V.," and he wore a blue polka-dot bandana knotted dashingly around his neck. His cavalryman's campaign hat was brim-pinned up on the left side with a huge regimental insignia of crossed sabers surmounted by the numeral 1.

Roosevelt was squat and bandy-legged, with pince-nez eyeglasses and black string fitted on a head that one writer irreverently likened to a pig-iron stewpot. The head, without

Colonel Theodore Roosevelt as he looked after the Santi-
ago Campaign—and much as he looked when he stepped
off the train in San Antonio in May, 1898.

benefit of neck, sat directly on his stiff brocade tunic collar. Thanking the well-wishers at the depot, Roosevelt congratulated Beck and his wilting bandsmen for their spirited rendition of "There'll Be a Hot Time in the Old Town Tonight," and joined Colonel Wood in a walk to the Menger Hotel for breakfast.

For his personal use, Roosevelt received handsome bay horses selected by his Texas friend John Moore, with whom T.R. once had hunted javelina on the Nueces River, and with characteristic display, rode one of them into the heart of the San Antonio business district. A large crowd gathered as he rode up and down St. Mary's Street several times.

At Camp Wood that evening, Roosevelt's tent became a

gathering place for well-wishers who began calling for a speech. The exuberant T.R. was happy to oblige. In his queerly raucous, excited voice, he proclaimed, "The eyes of the entire civilized world are upon you and I want your watch word to be 'Remember the *Maine*!' "

By May 17 the number of volunteers in the regiment had risen to nearly eight hundred; Riverside Park had been carefully measured off, tents erected neatly, the Exposition Building billets cleaned, and even the streets named. The Arizonans honored their Troop A captain by naming one "O'Neill Avenue." Other names included "Arizona Avenue," "Manila Avenue," and "Dewey Avenue," the last two to commemorate Admiral George Dewey's stunning May 1 victory over the Spanish fleet at Manila Bay—an event that gave Roosevelt special pleasure.

On the 17th, the Rough Riders were officially mustered in. The regiment consisted of three squadrons of four troops each: the Arizona Squadron, commanded by Major Brodie, had Troops A, B, and C from Arizona and Troop D from Oklahoma; the New Mexico Squadron, commanded by Major Henry Hersey, had four troops from New Mexico, lettered E, F, G, and H; and the third squadron was composed of Troops I, J, K, and L under Major George M. Dunn of Denver, Colorado.

Brodie's Arizonans broke down into Buckey's A Troop with three officers and sixty-eight men; Jim McClintock's Troop B with three officers and sixty-five men; and Captain Alexander's C Troop with three officers and sixty-seven men.

On May 23 the regiment drilled for the first time as a unit. Carbines and revolvers had been issued to all, helping to promote a truly military appearance, and selected troopers fired blank cartridges around the parade ground to teach the horses not to panic under gunfire. But, aside from the not altogether satisfactory regimental drill, the routine of the training period at Camp Wood seldom varied. Roosevelt at least once tried to vary it but ran into a rather rigid commanding officer as a result.

After one sultry afternoon of drilling, Roosevelt thought he would treat the men to refreshments to wash the San Antonio dust from their craws. He permitted the men to gulp all the beer they wanted—and picked up the tab. When Wood found out about it, he called his second in command to his tent and dressed Roosevelt down with a lecture on discipline. T.R.'s reaction was to tell Wood privately not long afterward, "I wish to say, sir, that I agree with what you said. I consider myself the damndest ass within ten miles of this camp."

Occasional passes were granted to the troopers. The escape from camp and the opportunity to crash a nearby *baile*, drink unsanctioned beer, or gawk at the girls was a welcome respite. The corpulent Professor Beck, Jim McClintock recalled, also figured in the camp's entertainment. Beck's chief joy, McClintock recalled, "was to come to the camp at the fairgrounds, take station before the colonel's tent, and noisily execute some stirring warlike composition just about the time the Colonel and his officers were in serious consultation."

On the night of May 25, Beck held a concern in the pavilion at Riverside Park, designed as a crowning touch to his musical contributions to the Rough Rider training period. The professor's band outdid itself in its martial spirit, and the *San Antonio Daily Light* reported that nearly everybody in town attended the festivities.

Toward the end of the program, band master Beck decided the most splendid military conclusion to his selections would be the playing of the "Cavalry Charge." He therefore instructed that at a propitious moment, on cue, a band member should shoot off a few blank shells with a small saluting cannon on the outskirts of the crowd. As the "Cavalry Charge" number reached a furious crecendo, Beck signaled and the cannon fired. A trooper instantly jumped out from the crowd and yelled, "Help him out, boys!" and soon several six-shooters and service revolvers added to the realism of the music. In the midst of the confusion, a stray bullet severed the electric light wire leading into the park, throwing the entire area into pitch darkness.

Ladies shrieked, children ducked under benches, waiters dropped trays of beer, and the well-oiled troopers laughed and
squeezed a few more shots off just for the hell of it.

The next day, the *Light* sanctimoniously described the whole
scene as "very disgraceful." The paper quoted Beck as saying
he had served in the Franco-Prussian War and had seen some
"hot times" but that he felt as uneasy in the pavillion as he ever
had in battle.

Beck's offering of favorite tunes not requiring gunfire punc-
tuation included "Arkansas Traveler," "Sweet Bye and Bye,"
"Good-bye, Dolly Gray," and "Dixie" and, dear to the hearts of
the "Mexican boys," was the bandmaster's versions of "Sobre
las Olas," and "La Paloma." But most often requested of the
good professor was the one tune everybody could sing along
with:

> When you hear
> Dem-a bells go ding, ling, ling;
> All join 'round
> And sweetly you must sing,
> And when the verse am through
> In the chorus all join in.
> THERE'LL BE A HOT TIME IN THE OLD TOWN TONIGHT!

The song became the unofficial anthem of the Rough Riders.

On May 27, Colonel Wood received long-awaited orders to
proceed to Tampa, Florida, where the regiment was to report
to Major General William R. Shafter, in command of the V
Corps of regulars and volunteers who were to take part in the
coming Cuban campaign. Next day the Rough Riders worked
at breaking camp, boxing and labeling supplies, striking tents,
and packing their gear. Told to be ready to leave on a moment's
notice, the troopers were issued three days' rations of hard tack,
corned beef, and coffee.

On Sunday, May 29, the troopers and officers rode through
ankle-deep dust out of Camp Wood to the San Antonio stock-
yards, where the train that was to carry them to Tampa was
being made up. The day was spent, until past midnight, getting

the recalcitrant horses aboard the stock cars. When the coaches for the men failed to arrive after the work was completed, many men trailed off to nearby saloons for a last few rounds of beer; some slept along the tracks until morning.

Just before the Rough Riders left San Antonio, Jim McClintock made a little presentation to his friend Buckey O'Neill. The gift was a black celluloid matchcase. Buckey's absorption of matches for his brown-paper fags had been a standing joke throughout Riverside Park, his usual salutation being "Jim, gimme a match," or "Ike, gimme a match."

Inside the matchcase, which McClintock had thoughtfully filled to capacity with wooden lucifers, Buckey placed a small slip of paper containing his name, rank, and home address.

CHAPTER TWENTY-FOUR

Chaos in Tampa

THE ROUGH RIDERS' train of stock and passenger cars made a memorable excursion of the Texas-to-Florida ride. At every stop in the Southland, where bitter memories of the War Between the States had kept wounds from healing for more than three decades, crowds large and small greeted the troopers and their officers, offering food and water, advice and conversation, asking answers to a million questions in return. In New Orleans, the volunteers mixed feeding their horses with feeding their eyes on a bevy of flirtatious young ladies who came out to greet them. Many troopers exchanged addresses with the belles, promising to write them from Cuba. In Tallahassee, some of McClintock's expert foragers appropriated several hogs found rooting in pens next to the tracks. When the station agent complained to Major Brodie, he ordered all the pigs returned to their owner. Tom Rynning said, "It sure was comical . . . to see that station agent strutting up and down the platform and telling his friends: 'Those sonsofbitches ain't going to get away with no hogs of mine.'"

The Tampa episode, while fortunately brief, presented a panoramic view of the logistical incompetence that characterized the Cuban operations of the Spanish-American War. The town itself lay on pine-covered flats at the end of a one-track railroad line, a miserable collection of shanties, sawgrass and sand dunes infested with clouds of bloodthirsty mosquitos and armies of spiders and centipedes. In contrasting splendor, the 13 minarets of the Tampa Bay Hotel stood in the distance. This bizarre structure, covering 6 acres and containing 500 rooms on 5 floors, became the principal gathering place for army officers and newspapermen, sipping mint julips and waving aside the 110-degree heat and humid, fetid air with palm-leaf fans on the great balconies. Roosevelt's friend, the dashing correpondent and "creative writer," Richard Harding Davis, referred to the Tampa Bay Hotel lounging as "the rocking-chair period of the war."

Since the hotel contained a fine gambling casino, Buckey O'Neill spent less than average time in the rocking chairs.

But few such pleasures could lessen the scene of utter chaos in Tampa at the time the Rough Riders arrived to join the regulars of Shafter's V Corps. The single-track railroad was so overtaxed that freight cars loaded with provisions, medicines, and materiel were backed up for miles. At one time three hundred cars loaded with war supplies were stalled along the track. Invoices and bills of lading were misplaced in the confusion, and the army had to break the seals on the cars to ascertain what they carried. Another day, fifteen cars loaded with lightweight uniforms were side-tracked twenty-five miles from Tampa while troopers suffered in the heat, wearing insufferable winter woolens. The stench of rotting meat in the stalled cars attracted dense swarms of green-bottle flies; the palmetto-overgrown sanddunes were littered with a bedlam of tents, piled packing crates, horse and mule remudas and attendant saddles, harness and forage; and on every point of the compass were thirty thousand drilling, milling soldiers, plus stevedores, newspapermen, government officials, camp followers, civilian gawkers, visitors, well-wishers, old soldiers, handshaking politicians, ladies, ship captains and sailors, and school children.

"Not in this world or the next," a Chicago reporter proclaimed with disbelief, "shall I see the equal of the mess at Tampa. I have seen sights at dock and railhead unmatched except in some huge lunatic asylum."

As a part of the V Corps, the Rough Riders' commander-in-chief was the gouty, three-hundred-pound Major General William Rufus Shafter of Kalamazoo, Michigan, who had estab-

lished himself in the Tampa Bay Hotel on April 29 after being
named to command the Cuban land expedition. He had served
in the Civil War with the Seventieth Michigan Infantry and
later with the Seventeenth and Forty-first Regular Infantry,
seeing service at Yorktown, West Point, Fair Oaks, Savage
Station, Glendale, and Malvern Hill. Ploddingly honest, Shafter
had great integrity. He also had more logistical problems than
he could handle. His outsized bulk made him a favorite of editorial cartoonists. He lacked in diplomacy, at times and, by
nature, was curt to the point of rudeness, a characteristic that
grated on the prima-donna sensibilities of reporters such as
Dick Davis.

More immediately, the Rough Riders came under the pep-
pery, hell-for-leather leadership of Brigadier General Joseph
"Fightin' Joe" Wheeler, who alongside Shafter, looked like a
cub beside the father bear. But size never meant much to
Wheeler. His somewhat frail-looking physique contained generous portions of guts and bundles of raw nerve ends, each
emitting its own perpetual charge of energy and driving him,
seemingly, in four directions at once. Sixty-two and an 1859
West Point graduate, he had fought with the Confederacy at
Shiloh, Murfreesboro, Chickamauga, and Knoxville; harassed
Sherman's army marching to Atlanta; opposed Rosecrans with
Bragg; commanded cavalry under Johnston and Hood; and
been under fire in an estimated eight hundred skirmishes and
battles. Robert E. Lee considered Wheeler one of the two best
cavalry men of the war—the other being the immortal J.E.B.
Stuart. After the war, Wheeler had settled in Wheeler, Ala-
bama, where he was admitted to the bar. Elected to Congress,
he had served eight terms by the time the War with Spain broke
out. Strongly favoring intervention in Cuba, Wheeler had made
many stirring speeches in the House expressing his mortifica-
tion that his Republican friends would openly admit fear of
armed conflict with Spain. "God forbid," he had said, "that the
growing generation should prefer to be money changers rather

than brave soldiers, fighting and if need be, dying, in the front rank of battle."

House Speaker Thomas B. "Czar" Reed once had commented that Wheeler would be around for a long time because "He never stays in one place long enough for God Almighty to put his finger on him." Though a strong Democrat, "Fightin' Joe" had refused to follow Cleveland's gold policies and had become a conspicuous silverite in the House. Given such attitudes and energy as he possessed, it is small wonder that he inspired in Buckey O'Neill a worship almost on a par with that which he accorded Wood and Roosevelt.

Wheeler commanded the cavalry division of Shafter's V Corps. More precisely, "Fightin' Joe" had a division composed of two brigades. The First Brigade included the Third, Sixth, and Ninth Cavalry regiments under Brigadier General S. S. Sumner; the Second Brigade included the First, Tenth (Negro), and First U.S. Volunteer Cavalry—the Rough Riders—all together under Brigadier General S. B. M. Young.

The lunatic-asylum atmosphere that obtained throughout the Tampa stay manifested itself nowhere more evidently than at Tampa Quay, where a group of nondescript steamers had anchored preparatory to transporting the 25,000 men of the V Corps to Cuba. Those transports that finally shouldered their way into Tampa Bay had a collective capacity of only 17,000 men. Thus necessity forced Shafter to order that each cavalry regiment could disembark only 8 of its 12 troops. Colonel Wood, in turn, decided to leave one troop from each of his first and second squadrons and two troops from the third behind in Tampa. The news was greeted with outrage by many of the volunteers who had worried all along that they might not "get in the war," and who, once they saw Florida, feared they would be left drilling on the palmetto, fighting mosquitos and flies "for the duration."

The thought of having to stay in Tampa for any length of time gagged not only the Rough Riders but also every other

trooper and infantryman there. Dysentery and fever were beginning to spread, and fresh fruit and vegetables were getting
scarce. One New York recruit expressed his disgust with the
place telling an eager reporter that on his first day in camp he
had been bitten by mosquitos, stung by a tarantula, felt a touch
of malaria, ran his bayonet into his hand, sat on an ant's nest,
stepped on an alligator, found a snake in his boot, and felt "like
a dirty deuce in a new deck." Even worse, there was little to
do besides clean a rifle, shine boots, or curry a horse. Ybor City,
a deadly little fever hole not far from Tampa, had a shooting
gallery and an opium den, and some of the troopers tried their
hand at both—shooting up the former with their revolvers until
the owner called the law. They emerged from the latter green
and puking and swearing never to touch even hard liquor again.

In brief, getting the hell out of Tampa became as great a concern as "getting in the war." Sergeant Tom Rynning of Mc-
Clintock's B Troop approached Buckey and explained that he
would join Buckey's troop as a private if he could go with him.
Buckey told him he would make a place for him if it came to
that. For Rynning it didn't come to that, but for many others
it did.

The final selection by Wood of those to remain behind in
Tampa included the whole of Captain Alexander's Troop C,
junior unit of the regiment, plus Troops H, I, and M under
Major Hersey of New Mexico.

To make bad matters worse, the Rough Riders had to leave
their pistols and horses in Tampa. The Regular Army men of
the Corps, more than a trifle jealous of the "privileges" extended
the volunteers, delighted in renaming the dismounted Rough
Rider's, "Wood's Weary Walkers."

On June 6, General Shafter received his orders from the War
Department "to capture the garrison at Santiago and assist in
capturing the harbor and fleet." He immediately ordered the
V Corps units to break camp and board the waiting steamers.

Colonel Wood boarded a launch and rode out to the *Yucatan*

before she docked to reserve space for his already depleted regiment. The *Yucatan*, an enormous, filthy commercial steamer, had been assigned to the Seventy-First Infantry— which Wood may or may not have known—but when a Seventy-First captain, A. J. Bleecker, and his soldiers came up to board her, they were greeted with a shower of coal from the Rough Riders, who had swarmed aboard the *Yucatan* the minute her gangplank hit the dock. Colonel Wallace A. Downs of the Seventy-First later decided to employ Wood and Roosevelt's commandeering tactics and took over the transport *Vigilancia* for his men.

When the gangplank was hauled back aboard, the *Yucatan* carried 33 officers and 578 men of the First U.S. Volunteer Cavalry Regiment plus 4 companies of the Second Infantry, a total of 773 enlisted men, each hunting a place to stow gear and await the time for landing on the Cuban beach. Unfortunately, the little armada was to swing at anchor for a week before getting underway; someone reported that the Spanish fleet had been sighted cruising off Key West, and the army could take no chances.

At last, on June 14, the thirty-two-vessel flotilla glided past the Dry Tortugas and through the Windward Passage to the Caribbean Sea. A water-tank ship wallowing in tow held the fleet to a snail's pace. A speed of seven knots, slow enough, often had to be reduced, sometimes to near zero.

Aboard the *Yucatan*, nearly 900 men huddled in a ship with an utmost capacity of 750. Early in the voyage a trooper hung out a huge hand-made sign announcing "Standing Room Only." Another soon amended it to read "And Damn Little of That." Men accustomed to the hurricane deck of a Western bronc or the lustrously groomed back of a polo pony were quickly pasty-faced with seasickness. In the multiple tiers of bunks in the hold of the *Yucatan* there was no solace. Lying like sardines in cramped and fetid air, most braved the pitching and heaving on deck rather than the claustrophobic atmosphere below.

" . . . jammed together under the tropical sun on these crowded troop ships," Roosevelt later wrote angrily, "we are in a sewer."

Cans of the stringy, clotted, nauseatingly greasy beef in the hold ruptured and soon began emitting a stench that permeated every square inch of the wallowing vessel. Wood ordered the entire lot pitched overboard. Rough Rider Tom Hall observed, "Dumped overboard in sufficient quantities and at proper points it would reform the entire breed of man-eating sharks and add abundantly to the peace and comfort of a much perturbed world."

Body lice, bane of soldiers in unclean quarters in all wars, plagued the ships. Many men tied their uniforms on lines and dragged them in the water to rid them of vermin. And, on top of it all, the drinking water began to taste badly about half way through the 5½-day voyage. Only with grimacing effort could the officers maintain their dignity and hoist a toast of the tepid, stinking water: "May the war last until each is killed, wounded or promoted."

Buckey, during the voyage to Cuba, got to know and like the young acting surgeon of the regiment, Dr. Robb Church, a former Princeton football player destined to win the Medal of Honor in the forthcoming campaign. Roosevelt, with amazement, later recalled Buckey and Dr. Church talking over "Aryan root-words together and then sliding off into a review of the novels of Balzac."

Roosevelt, on the *Yucatan* voyage, perhaps more than at any other time, also became acquainted with his officers. In the book on his regiment to be published the next year, he wrote often, fondly, and with introspection about the one man he seemed to admire above nearly all the others of his Western volunteers:

Most of the men had simple souls. They could relate facts, and they said very little about what they dimly felt. Buckey O'Neill, however, the iron-nerved, iron-willed fighter from Arizona, the sheriff whose name was a byword of terror to every wrong-doer, white or red, the gambler who with unmoved face would stake and lose every dollar he had in the world—he, alone with his comrades, was a visionary, an articulate emotionalist. He was very quiet about it, never talking unless he was sure of his listener; but at night when we leaned upon the railing to look at the Southern Cross, he was less apt to tell tales of his hard and stormy past than he was to speak of the mysteries which lie behind courage, and fear, and love.

At daybreak on June 20, the rugged peaks of the Sierra Maestra range were discernible through the morning fog as the flotilla rendezvoused with Admiral Sampson's fleet in a semicircular blockade off the mouth of Santiago Harbor. Shafter's ships lay in wait, beyond the distant and ominous sentry of the imposing Morro Castle, where the newspapers had reported so many horrible tortures and unspeakable acts had found headquarters. A gig took the general to Sampson's flagship *Brooklyn*, there to coordinate efforts for the reduction of the city of Santiago de Cuba, the chief objective of both the naval and land expeditions.

On the morning of June 22, Shafter's steamers arrived at their debarkation point, a squalid little village named Daiquiri, sixteen miles east of the Santiago Harbor mouth.

CHAPTER TWENTY-FIVE

Daiquiri and Las Guasimas

THE LANDING AT DAIQUIRI could have been only a chapter of the Spanish-American War. Separated from it and described in all its hectic, play-it-by-ear, blind-luck splendor, it fits nowhere else in the military history of America. The landing boats bobbed and swung in the vicious swells between the transports and Daiquiri's rickety steel-and-wood pier. As the boats neared the outjutting dock, the troopers had to time themselves precisely: when the boat rode the crest of a swell, the men grabbed the wooden stringpieces of the pier and hoisted themselves upon it with main strength. The boats meantime bobbed like corks on the heaving sea. Many of them were smashed to kindling against the slimy pilings.

Buckey stood on the loose planking of the jetty in the early afternoon of June 22, first day of the landing, trying to bring order out of the nightmarishly dangerous sea circus called the V Corps debarkation. As he shouted orders and pulled men from the slamming gunwhales of their boats onto the dock, a boatload of Negro troopers from the Tenth Cavalry attempted to make contact with the pier. Two of these "buffalo soldiers," Private John English of Chattanooga, Tennessee, and Corporal Edward Cobb of Richmond, Virginia, slipped in climbing from their lighter and instantly disappeared in the frothing sea, sucked beneath the pier supports. Buckey, fully clothed, leaped into the water in a heroic if rash effort to bring the men, weighted with blanket rolls and cartridge belts, to the surface, but he could find no trace of either.

There were no other human casualties in the Daiquiri landing, but six horses died trying to swim ashore. Many of the
horses and pack animals had been thrown overboard into the
terrible, pounding surf as the simplest and most expedient way
of getting them ashore. When a group of cavalry mounts began
to swim from the ships toward the open sea, a quick-thinking
bugler on the beach blew the proper call, and the horses wheeled
and headed for shore. Roosevelt himself encountered the greatest
of difficulties in getting his two horses ashore (only top cavalry
officers had been permitted to take their mounts on the transports) and supervised their unloading with growing perplexity.
The first broke through its belly-band as it was hoisted from
the transport and fell into the sea and drowned; the second was
the victim of too much tender loving care. As Roosevelt snorted,
spit and cussed, the crewmen delicately lifted the beast an inch
at a time on the hoist, discussing every foot of distance ani-
matedly until Roosevelt, red-faced and beside himself with
rage, shouted "Stop that goddamned animal torture!" At last
lowered into the water, the horse splashed ashore unharmed.

At least part of the landing problem lay in the refusal of the
transport captains to bring their vessels closer to shore. Richard
Harding Davis, who had developed a keen dislike for Shafter to
begin with (the general had bluntly told Davis he "didn't give
a damn" if Davis *was* a "creative writer," he could expect no
special privileges), watched the landing with smoldering rage.
Davis, laying the blame for the spectacle directly at the door-
step of the civilian ship captains, wrote with a short fuse for
Scribner's:

. . . [the] transport captains acted with an independence and in disregard of what was required of them, that should, early in the day,
have led to their being placed in irons. . . . In a word, they acted
entirely on what they believed to be the interest of the "Owners,"
meaning not the Government. which was paying them enormous
rents per day, but the men who employed them in time of peace. For
the greater part of each day these men kept from three to twenty
miles out at sea, where it was impossible to communicate with them.
. . . I was on six different transports. and on none of them did I find

a captain who was, in his attitude toward the Government, anything but insolent, un-American and mutinous.

Some of the first Rough Riders ashore, on instructions from Roosevelt and apparently on the basis of an idea of the *New York Journal* correspondent Edward Marshall, headed for the blockhouse on Mount Losiltires, just east of the landing point, to raise the regimental colors—the flag presented to Major Brodie in Prescott by the Women's Relief Corps of Phoenix. Color Sergeant Albert P. Wright of Yuma, with the help of a civilian sailor, managed to lash the colors to the blockhouse staff.

By nightfall about six thousand men had landed, including the entire foreshortened Rough Rider regiment. Buckey and Kennett Harris of the *Chicago Record* climbed the hill behind the town to the still-smoking ruins of a railroad roundhouse the Spanish had burned before evacuating the area. Little remained of the village. Struck by shelling from Sampson's warships and set afire by the Spaniards, it appeared as still-smoking ruins, with only a few palm-thatched huts still standing. Few natives remained behind, and there were no signs of the enemy but devastation.

One thing was clear to reporters such as Harris who examined Daiquiri village: had the enemy possessed the leadership, imagination, and simple desire to fight common to most invaded countries, they easily could have wiped out the entire American landing force during the Daiquiri beachhead.

Thus, while newspaper artist Frederic Remington, aboard one of the transports, said "We held our breath. We expected a most desperate fight for the landing," not a single enemy shot was fired.

The landing continued until two o'clock on the morning of June 23 with *Scribner's* man Dick Davis fulfilling his self-proclaimed title of "creative writer" by writing from the Rough Rider encampment:

It was one of the most weird and remarkable scenes of the war, probably of any war. An army was being landed on an enemy's coast at the dead of night, but with somewhat more of cheers and shrieks and laughter than rise from the bathers in the surf at Coney Island on a hot Sunday. It was a pandemonium of noise. The men still to be landed from the "prison hulks," as they called the transports, were singing in chorus, the men already on the shore were dancing naked around the campfires on the beach, or shouting with delight as they plunged into the first bath that offered in seven days, and those in the launches as they were pitched head-first at the soil of Cuba, signalized their arrival by howls of triumph. On either side rose black overhanging ridges, in the lowland between were white tents and burning fires, the dazzling eyes of the searchlights shaming the quiet moonlight.

The first night ashore, the Rough Riders bivouacked along a jungle roadway, a few miles inland from the beach, fearful, as Remington had been, of a sneak Spanish attack. The night's sleep was fitful, troopers awakening suddenly to the scuttlings of the huge, obscene, orchid-colored land crabs that infested Cuban beaches, and to the clouds of mosquitos—carriers of malaria—that periodically descended to harass man and beast alike.

The sole reason for sending Shafter's V Corps to Cuba in the first place was to support Admiral Sampson, enabling the navy to enter Santiago Harbor and capture or destroy the Spanish fleet at anchor there. The strength of the Spanish Army in the province of Santiago was something over 36,000 troops with about 10,000 of them in and around the city of Santiago and its well-fortified harbor. Shafter's plan was to make a quick-plunging drive toward Santiago by the most direct route, by the one road leading from Daiquiri to the town of Siboney, a yellow-fever pesthole some 10 miles westward along the coast. He then would strike northwestward to the convergence of roads called Las Guasimas, about 15 miles southeast of the eastern approaches to Santiago.

On June 23, Brigadier General Henry W. Lawton, commanding the vanguard of troops, reached Siboney and captured it without difficulty, establishing a defense perimeter behind the beach so that the better facilities of the Siboney beach, as well

as Daiquiri, could be used for further debarkation. While
Lawton engaged in organizing this defense, Fightin' Joe
Wheeler stole a march on him and pushed on toward Las Gua-
simas with his dismounted cavalry division that included the
Rough Riders.

Las Guasimas was Wheeler's show from the start. Early on
June 24 he ordered Brigadier General S.B.M. Young's brigade
of the First and Tenth Regular Cavalry on the main road from
Siboney to Santiago. Colonel Wood's First Volunteer Cavalry
was to thread its way along the steep and difficult trail parallel-
ing Young's route of march to the left. The two units were to
converge at Las Guasimas.

The opening shot of the first land engagement of the Santiago
campaign occurred at 8:15 that morning when the Rough
Riders and Young's brigade—totaling 964 men—ran into the
rear guard of a retiring Spanish force of some 1,500 soldiers.
Enemy sniper fire crackled through the trees and brush from
well-camouflaged positions. In the exchange of fire, leaves and
twigs fell from trees in a shower. The Spanish, volley-firing
from entrenched and well-concealed positions along the crest of
a 250-foot ridge that commanded the trails, were producing
casualties among Wheeler's force—including some of the key
Rough Rider officers.

Jim McClintock, anxious to throw his B Troop into the
skirmish and fearing it would all end before he could take part,
had just placed his troopers in the skirmish line when he was
bowled over by two Mauser shots striking him in the lower left
leg. McClintock propped himself against a tree, shaken, his
boot filling with blood, to await medical aid. In a few minutes
a husky private, William B. Proffit of Prescott, found the B
Troop captain and began carrying him piggyback toward the
rear. Along the way, Sergeant Tom Rynning met the two and
asked McClintock if he had any last orders. The captain's reply
was simply "Give 'em hell."

Meantime, Major Brodie prepared to launch an attack on the
Spanish right flank and to protect his men from a possible

countermove. He ordered Troops D and E into position to secure his left flank. Brodie was just moving his squadron ahead when a sniper shot smashed into his right forearm, shattering the bone and spinning the lanky West Pointer to the ground. Later, Wood would describe to *New York Journal* correspondent

Captain James H. McClintock, commanding Troop B of the Rough Riders. This photo of Buckey's close friend was taken in Cuba the day before McClintock was wounded at Las Guasimas (photo courtesy Los Angeles County Museum of Natural History).

Edward Marshall, one of three correspondents who accompanied the Rough Riders to Las Guasimas, Brodie's predicament:

Brodie had not the least idea that he could be hit by a mere Spaniard. I shall never forget his expression of amazement and anger as he hopped down the hill on one foot with the other in the air, before he fell. He came toward me, shouting, "Great Scott, colonel, they've *hit* me!

With Brodie now out of action, Roosevelt took command of his squadron, but the final charge through the dense brush met only desultory fire from the retreating Spanish soldiers.

The fight at Las Guasimas took something less than three hours but cost the lives of fifteen Americans—including eight Rough Riders.

Like Brodie and McClintock—and Buckey O'Neill in a fateful later moment—Roosevelt and Wood disdained the Spanish bullets with foolhardy coolness. Jesse D. Langdon, one of Woodbury Kane's K Troopers, later reflected, "At no time during combat did I see Teddy Roosevelt or Wood in a prone position. Both of these officers stood up at all times to observe the deployment of troops and the enemy through binoculars."

To some writers, Las Guasimas was a signal American victory with the Rough Riders taking the most exaggerated praise for gallantry and dauntless courage under fire. To some others, the encounter was an ambush with the Rough Riders the victims. In the latter group was Stephen Crane of the *New York World*. While tending, like so many of the correspondents, to place Roosevelt in command of the unit, *The Red Badge of Courage* author filed the following story to the *World* following the little battle:

PLAYA DEL ESTE, June 24—Lt. Col. Roosevelt's Rough Riders, who were ambushed yesterday, advanced at daylight without any particular plan of action as to how to strike the enemy.

The men marched noisily through the narrow road in the woods, talking volubly, when suddenly they struck the Spanish lines.

Fierce fire was poured into their ranks and there began a great fight in the thickets.

Nothing of the enemy was visible to our men, who displayed much gallantry. In fact, their bearing was superb and couldn't have been finer.

They suffered a heavy loss, however, due to the remarkably wrong idea of how the Spanish bushwhack.

It was simply a gallant blunder.

Dick Davis, writing for the *New York Herald*, also indicated at first that the Rough Riders had been ambushed but later explained that there was a great difference in blundering into an ambush and knowing beforehand that the enemy would attempt to ambush. The controversy over Crane's and other first reports on the Las Guasimas "gallant blunder" would rage on throughout the quick little war. Roosevelt simply said,

. . . our line never went back ten yards in any place, and the advance was practically steady; while an hour and a half after the fight began we were in complete possession of the entire Spanish position, and their troops were fleeing in masses down the road, our men being too exhausted to follow them. . . . As it was, with a force half of regulars and half of volunteers, we drove out a superior number of Spanish regular troops, strongly posted, without suffering a very heavy loss.

After a brief encounter, Buckey and Colonel Roosevelt personally went over the ground to count the dead and check on the wounded. In a short time, the swollen corpses exposed along the trail attracted the hideous purple crabs and in some cases even more nightmarish jungle vultures. Buckey had just inspected the mutilated body of Corporal George H. Doherty, a big miner from Jerome, Arizona, and a member of Buckey's own troop, when he turned to Roosevelt and asked: "Colonel, isn't it Whitman who says of the vultures that 'they pluck the eyes of princes and tear the flesh of kings'?"

With a few days' rest before moving up for the assault on Santiago, Buckey found time to write a few letters, handle some correspondence for his wounded Arizona comrades Brodie and McClintock, and even to begin, of all things, a regimental raffle to help the widow of Captain Allyn Capron of Troop L, killed

in the Las Guasimas battle. Lieutenant Tom Hall, attached to
Wood's staff as adjutant, later wrote of Buckey's idea concern-
ing the raffling of Captain Capron's horse: "He expected to be
able to send Captain Capron's widow several hundred dollars
for the horse and then give her the horse." Hall added that he
considered Captain O'Neill "all wool and a yard wide."

Hall claimed that Buckey, in the waiting period between Las
Guasimas and the Santiago offensive, developed some ideas of
staying in Cuba after the war ended. "O'Neill was the most in-
defatigable schemer that ever was," Hall commented. "He already had a number of mining companies projected to develop
the wealth of Cuba, to say nothing of sugar companies and huge
cattle ranches which were sure to prove money winners because
of the never ending supply of grass and water."

The adjutant also remembered that Buckey had broached the
idea of an association for the Rough Riders after the war. Buckey
wanted to call it the "Military Order of the Morro," and Hall
said he approached Colonel Wood on the idea. Wood, in turn,
suggested "The Military Order of the Foreign Wars of the Republic," decidedly a less choice name. Buckey's idea eventually
became recognized as the genesis for the "Rough Rider's Association."

Casualties among the Rough Riders at Las Guasimas amounted
to 8 dead and 34 wounded.[9] The First Regular Cavalry lost 7
killed and 8 wounded; the Tenth lost 1 man killed, 10 wounded.
Out of the 964 Americans engaged, 16 were killed, 52 wounded.
On the Spanish side, the casualties were never officially agreed
upon, but they were believed considerably less than the American losses, with 1,500 men engaged.

The Las Guasimas clash gave the V Corps a new staging area,
five miles closer to Santiago, with adequate camping area and
good water. A few miles west of the Rough Riders' position, on
the hillside across the San Juan River valley, the Spanish were
digging in. A trench could be seen opening up in the long ridge

---

[9] It is interesting to note that among the wounded at Las Guasimas was a trum-
peter from Muskogee, Indian Territory, named Thomas F. Meagher, the same as
the man with whom Buckey's father served at Fredericksburg.

complex, also called San Juan, as workmen, their straw som-
breros bobbing up and down, worked furiously to finish it
before the expected American attack.

Richard Harding Davis, who had received an almost un-
precedented honor by being named in Roosevelt's official dispatches for his part in helping the Rough Riders sight the enemy
at Las Guasimas, watched the work and saw blue-coated Spanish
officers strolling leisurely about and riding over the hillsides on
little white ponies. "The rifle pits were growing in length,"
Davis jotted in his notebook, "and in plain sight of the hill of
El Poso, the enemy was intrenching itself at San Juan and at
the little village of El Caney."

On June 26, Buckey wrote a letter to Pauline, a cheerful,
short, hastily scribbled note containing only the briefest mention of the war, and assuring her that he was all right and was
sorry to be so hurried but had to help bury the dead.

CHAPTER TWENTY-SIX

Up to Kettle Hill

BUCKEY AND HIS TROOPERS waited in a drumming rain at their bivouac near Sevilla, two miles northeast of Las Guasimas, which had been selected by General Shafter as his headquarters. The rain poured through the jungle growth, turning the trails to porridge, running in rivulets off shelter tents, hissing into campfires but cleansing the air and affording a brief respite from the enervating heat of the jungle.

Down the single, sunken wagon road from Las Guasimas, six days were being required to bring troops and materiel to Shafter's command post for the soon-to-be launched Santiago offensive. Rations again were scarce, and even the hardtack staple was becoming inedible—soaked with muddy water leaking through the wooden crates. The bacon seemed slimy and the salt pork tainted, and the canned beans nauseating in their pool of pork grease; the cans of beef, which some troopers claimed made the vultures puke, rusted untouched. Even the coffee beans were green; pounded to pulp in a cheesecloth with the butt of a pistol or rock, the brew was barely drinkable after stewing in an iron coffeepot for hours. Worst of all, particularly for a classic addict like Buckey O'Neill, was the scarcity of tobacco, and a seasoned forager could come up with little more than a native plug, worth eight cents, for less than two dollars.

Captain O'Neill had no reputation among his men as a disciplinarian. He was easy-going and seemed embarrassed at the salutes, snappier now with experience, thrown his way and at the staccatoed "sirs" that punctuated sentences addressed to him by men whom he had known for years in Arizona Territory and who had never called him anything but "Buckey." Thus, the few days between the Las Guasimas battle and the coming march toward Santiago were dutiless among O'Neill's troopers. Most huddled in shelters out of the rain, emerging only when required to stand guard, go on outpost duty, scout out a trail or rumor, or run messages to Wood and Roosevelt. A few occasionally stripped naked to bathe in the downpour.

Adjutant Tom Hall, knowing something of Buckey's spectacular career in Arizona as lawman, politician, and mining magnate, developed a strong friendship for the captain. Hall bummed from Buckey one of the colored hat bands the Troop A men had received before leaving Prescott. He then sent the band to a lady friend, with a letter explaining who was the owner of this "priceless souvenir." Apparently the lady had a special appreciation for heroes—Buckey's exploit in trying to save the Negro troopers at Daiquiri had been well advertised in the national press—and wrote Hall that she had put the band around a bust of Napoleon. Hall relayed this message to Captain O'Neill and, to Buckey's delight, explained that his lady friend considered the band "the proudest decoration Napoleon ever wore."

On the last day of June, Shafter's V Corps began moving into position for the assault on Santiago's most important eastward defenses, the series of ridges known collectively as the San Juan Heights, and the fortified village of El Caney, to the north. Shafter reconnoitered the Siboney-Santiago road as far as a small hill above the abandoned ranch called El Poso, just west of the Rough Riders' bivouac. The commander's plan involved preventing the reinforcement of Santiago and cutting the town's water supply by taking the strongly garrisoned Caney position first. A frontal assault on the San Juan Ridge complex would follow. General Lawton, commanding a force of 6,000 men, nearly half of Shafter's command, was to take El Caney, a position commanded by a stone church slotted with loopholes, where Hernán Cortés is said to have prayed before setting sail for

Mexico in 1519. Major General Jacob F. Kent had been selected
to command the infantry forces on the San Juan operation, accompanied by General Wheeler's dismounted cavalry division
and three batteries of artillery, a total of about 8,400 men and
officers.

Late on the afternoon of June 30, the Rough Riders drew
three days' rations and formed up in troops. The regiment then
marched westward to El Poso Ranch, where the road from
Siboney sliced through along the Aguadores River, about a mile
and a half behind the San Juan Heights. The troopers reached
El Poso just after dark and camped along the roadway to eat by
flickering campfires.

Reveille sounded for the V Corps at dawn on July 1. From the
start the day threatened to be a scorcher, with high humidity
from the rains two days previously. The Rough Rider camp
bustled with activity. After breakfast some of the troopers
climbed the ridge above El Poso, where Shafter previously had
reconnoitered, to look at the Spanish lines looping out across
the valley on San Juan Heights, dimly seen through the morning mist.

Two significant changes had occurred in the volunteers' command chain. General Joe Wheeler, stricken with fever and
racked with chills, had sent Brigadier General Samuel S. Sumner to take command of the cavalry division; and Colonel Wood,
elevated to Second Brigade command by the illness of S. B. M.
Young, had relinquished his command of the First Volunteer
Cavalry to his eager friend, Theodore Roosevelt, who was made
a full colonel.

As the sun boiled away the morning fog, Buckey received
orders from Roosevelt to move his Troop A from El Poso down
the ridge, closer to the eastward approaches to Santiago Harbor.
His position was to prevent a surprise attack from that flank.
Buckey sent ahead a scouting party of twelve troopers and by
seven o'clock the men occupied their new positions on the ridge
east of the harbor. From these heights, they could see the har-

bor's glistening turquoise-blue waters to their left, the bright ribbon of the Aguadores River and the imposing San Juan Heights to their right. On the latter, rising sharply from the jungle beyond the river, the enemy fortifications were clearly visible.

At about the time Buckey's troop took over their new positions, the deep-throated boom of artillery fire reverberated from El Caney, to the north. And, at the same moment, the battery of Hotchkiss revolving cannon opened a chattering fire on the San Juan entrenchments and fortifications. At first the Spanish forces did not respond to the artillery pieces, pounding round after round into their breastworks. Then, as the fire was returned, a hail of shrapnel poured into the El Poso position, where the Grimes Battery position was marked by a fog of black smoke.

Roosevelt and his regiment, their El Poso positions endangered, received permission to cross the Aguadores and seek cover in the jungle growth beyond. Some of the troopers simply ran for cover without awaiting instructions, dumping packs and blanket rolls along the way, scrambling down the slopes toward the San Juan River. The narrow trails were congested with infantrymen, wounded and lost. The undergrowth was so thick that the soldiers could not move off the trails; they were reduced to a jostling, anxious, angry crowd trying to move against a wave of equally anxious and angry men going the other way.

In crossing the Aguadores River, the Rough Riders narrowly escaped mass casualties when, near the ford, a Signal Corps balloon, dragged into position by ground anchoring ropes, swayed above the treetops and attracted a hail of Spanish sniper fire. The bullets not only ripped into the balloon—which Stephen Crane described as "huge, fat, yellow, and quivering" —but also into the mass of troops below, jammed along the roadway. Outraged, General Wood noted in his diary that the dragging forward of the elephantine observation bag "was one of the most ill-judged and idiotic acts that I have witnessed."

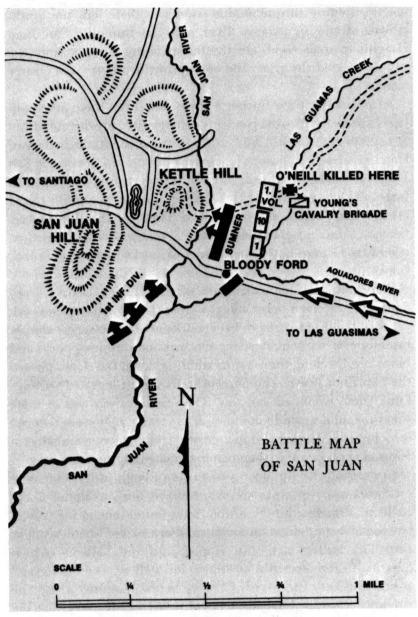

Battle positions on July 1, 1898 (by permission from THE ARIZONA
ROUGH RIDERS, *Charles Herner, Tucson, University of Arizona Press,
copyright 1970).*

The balloon, before being torn to shreds by the volley firing of the Spaniards, did manage to locate an unused trail that helped relieve the congestion near the ford.

After crossing the hip-deep Aguadores, the Rough Riders marched about three-quarters of a mile northward, as Buckey's Troop A returned to bring up the rear. They assumed a new position in a sunken roadway along Las Guamas Creek, half a mile in front of a small hill upon which sat an abandoned sugar mill and two large refining kettles. The troopers dubbed it "Kettle Hill." Perhaps a quarter mile beyond it loomed the higher knolls of the San Juan Heights, separated from Kettle Hill by a narrow valley and a small lake, thick jungle growth, and a few scattered tall palms. San Juan Hill, topped by a formidable blockhouse, stood to the left of Kettle in easy view, the Siboney-Santiago road almost bisecting it on its northern slope.

Kettle Hill itself contained heavy fortifications and was laced with entrenchments. Volleys of rifle fire from the sugar-mill ruins poured down on the Rough Riders in an intermittant hail. Mauser bullets whizzed and rustled between the meadow grass and tree leaves that separated the First Volunteer Cavalry from the black regulars of the Ninth Cavalry, in the positions ahead of them. Returning the sniper fire was not permitted because of the troopers in front and the distance to the Spanish positions, deemed too great for any purposeful firing—particularly since the Spanish were expertly concealed and using smokeless powder.

It was now midmorning and the fire from Kettle Hill inevitably began inflicting casualties. The dead were left where they fell, the wounded who could attract medical aid drawn back to the streams, where they were laid in rows, feet touching the water's edge, bodies supported by the muddy banks.

"The noise of the Mauser bullet," wrote correspondent Edward Marshall, "is not impressive enough to be really terrifying until you have seen what it does when it strikes. It is a nasty, malicious little noise, like the soul of a very petty and

mean person turned into sound." And Marshall knew what he
was talking about. During the Las Guasimas action a Mauser
bullet had struck him in the spine. A surgeon told him flatly
that he could not live. Although Marshall lost a leg, he lived
to write a book about the Rough Riders.

During the nervous period of waiting below Kettle Hill, while
the "nasty and malicious" Mauser bullets continued to hum
and whine and thin the American ranks, one could sense the
crawling fear among the volunteers. Unable to shoot back, unable to move, they cringed under cover, in view of the poncho-
covered bodies under trees and the wounded straggling back
toward the river, hoping a stray sniper shot would not find its
mark.

Buckey hoped at least to give a sense of reassurance to his
men. Neither Roosevelt, Brodie, McClintock, nor Captain
O'Neill had shown much sense of self-preservation when it
came to enemy fire. At Las Guasimas, Buckey had scared everybody in sight with his fearless, reckless, even foolhardy, disdain
for Spanish gunfire. But Wood and Roosevelt, toward whom
every trooper and officer looked for example, did the same thing.
Brodie could not believe he could be hit—until he was. Thus,
Buckey's striding in front of his troopers was not so conscious
an act, either at Las Guasimas or before Kettle Hill, as it was
a result of disdain for the Spaniards and a feeling that it be-
hooved a commanding officer to reassure his men.

The fire from the Kettle Hill positions poured down unceas-
ingly along the roadway and sunken lane, occasionally pinging
off the barbed-wire strands of the fence strung along the road
on both sides, thudding into the fence posts, tree trunks, and
ground, neatly snipping leaves and twigs from the trees.

As Buckey paced in front of his waiting troopers, occasionally
stopping long enough to twist a new cigarette from borrowed
tobacco, Lieutenant Woodbury Kane, whose Troop K was deployed nearby, warned his superior officer to take cover. But,
like Alex Brodie, Buckey felt he owed his men the confidence

of his own fearlessness and contempt for the Spanish soldier while they were under fire.

Buckey's disdain for the Spanish soldier, and Brodie's, was an attitude endemic in military as well as civilian ranks. Buckey more than once had said, half-jokingly, "The Spanish bullet is not molded that will kill me."

At about ten o'clock the morning of July 1, 1898, Buckey strolled over to talk with Captain Robert D. Howze, an aide to General Sumner. The conversation ended abruptly a few minutes later as a Mauser bullet, fired aimlessly by the enemy, struck Buckey in the head with a chilling "splat." Captain O'Neill crumpled to the earth without a sound.

CHAPTER TWENTY-SEVEN

Death Was the Black Horse

 THERE CAN BE little argument over the circumstances of Buckey O'Neill's death, despite the fact that the recorded testimony, though ample, is sometimes varied.

Second Lieutenant Joshua D. Carter of Buckey's Troop A, a Prescott officer two years younger than his captain, set the time at ten A.M., observing that "Captain O'Neill was constitutionally opposed to getting under cover." At the moment death came, Buckey was talking to Captain Howze some fifteen feet from his crouching troopers. Private Jesse Langdon of Woodbury Kane's K Troop saw precisely what happened and recalls it vividly:

I was not a member of his troop, however I actually saw him die as I was not fifty feet from him, and the attention of everyone near him was called to him by the fact that everyone was telling him to "lay down" . . . at that moment he was hit in the mouth, the bullet coming out the back of his head.

Private Arthur Tuttle of Safford, a member of Buckey's troop, also heard the murmur of Buckey's and Howze's conversation. Tuttle recalled that he was staring straight at Captain O'Neill when he saw his commander stiffen and collapse without a sound. "I heard the bullet," Tuttle later recounted; "you usually can if you're close enough, you know. It makes a sort of 'spat.' He was dead before he hit the ground."

One William Pulsing told a *New York Times* reporter two months afterward that he too was an eyewitness to the tragedy: "Suddenly a Mauser bullet struck him squarely in the mouth," Pulsing said, "going in so evenly that his teeth weren't injured.

He fell to the ground at once, and I and a man named Boyle[10] who was afterward killed in battle, picked him up and carried his body to the rear. He died there in a few seconds."

As Buckey fell, everyone in the vicinity ran toward him. Two troopers pulled his body to shelter in a small depression under some trees and placed his campaign hat over his face. Lieutenant Frank Frantz, Buckey's second in command, was especially distraught as he rushed to the captain's body. Then, hands bloody, Frantz flew down the road, uselessly searching for a doctor.

Private A. D. Webb, another Safford member of Troop A, wrote, "The death of Captain O'Neill seemed to paralyze the troop as no one appeared to know what to do . . . each man in the troop started out to do a little fighting on his own account to get even with the Spanish."

A detail of troopers buried the captain in a necessarily hasty and shallow grave in the meadow near where he had fallen, there to await the end of the war. "No person was there to tell of the nobleness of his character and his funeral dirge was the whistle of bullets and the scream of shells," Trooper Webb wrote. "Buckey is dead, but death will close the eyes of the last trooper who fought under him 'ere he is forgotten.' "

Roosevelt, informed of Buckey's death, was greatly saddened. "Even before he fell," the Rough Riders' colonel later wrote, "his wild and gallant soul had gone out into the darkness."

Adjutant Tom Hall heard the news and rushed to the site where Buckey's body lay awaiting burial. Hall recalled the incident of the ribbon hat band Buckey had donated to Hall's lady friend, and the delight the captain had expressed on learning that the souvenir decorated a bust of Napoleon. ". . . When I passed by his body," Hall wrote, ". . . and stooped to raise the hat from his poor head, I couldn't read any satisfaction in the glazed eyes that looked back at me. He was of the type whose

10 This was James Boyle of Carbon County, Pennsylvania, a resident of Prescott, thirty-one years old, and a member of Troop A. Boyle was wounded in the neck and body at San Juan on July 1 and died of his wounds the following day.

soldierly fault is their useless bravery—a knight of chivalry in
the dirty brown jeans of a Rough Rider."

Few besides Pauline, who would not learn of her husband's
death until several days later, would remember Buckey's own
words on death. He had written, in the short story "A Horse of
the Hash-Knife Brand,"

After all the Indians were right. Death was the black horse that came
some day into every man's camp, and no matter when that day came
a brave man should be booted and spurred and ready to ride him out.

The Rough Riders stormed Kettle Hill recklessly and deter-
minedly on the afternoon following Buckey's death. Due in
large measure to the work of a Gatling-gun detachment under
command of Captain John Parker, the entire San Juan complex
had fallen to the Americans by two-thirty.

Casualties in the July 1 battle amounted to a total of 50 officers and more than 500 men killed and wounded. Of the 490
Rough Riders who had answered muster at El Poso on the morning of July 1, 11 were dead and 65 wounded by nightfall. Four
of the wounded would die and 2 men would be killed and 11
more wounded the next day, as fighting on the San Juan ridges
came to an end.

Trooper Jesse Langdon of Troop K gives an extraordinary
account of the final assault on San Juan:

. . . you will note that he (Roosevelt) gave more credit to Capt. Parker
than any other man for taking San Juan Hill. Parker's Gatling guns
killed practically every Spanish soldier who raised his head to fire
from the trenches. This accounts for the fact that so few Spanish
bullets found our troops.

Langdon[11] also writes to the present author:

As a matter of fact, "Buckey" was the only man whom I actually saw
killed by a Spanish bullet, and I saw many die to my right and left,
struck from the rear by fifty caliber bullets fired by the 71st N.Y.
Militia who followed us up Kettle and San Juan Hills. The members
of the 71st who followed us up to the Spanish trenches, when ques-

[11] Langdon, of Red Hook, New York, is the last surviving member of the Rough
Riders.

Jesse D. Langdon, the last Rough Rider, eyewitness to Captain O'Neill's death below Kettle Hill on July 1, 1898 (photo taken in 1972 by Alvin Spencer Fick).

tioned, explained that they thought members of the U.S. Cavalry regulars who were wearing sky blue capes lined with bright orange, were retreating Spanish officers. This was proved to some extent by the fact that nearly all of those wearing capes were picked off before reaching the Spanish entrenchments. The 71st proved that they were good marksmen.

Charles Herner, historian of the Arizona volunteers, says:

The Arizonans were proud of the record they made at San Juan. Composed of five officers and one hundred and thirty-six men on the morning of July 1, the two Arizona troops made up approximately one-fourth of the effective fighting force of the Regiment. Yet, out of the fifteen Rough Riders who died from wounds received that day— eight were in the Arizona troops.

Buckey O'Neill was the only regimental officer killed among the Arizona volunteers. Sixty-seven days before he died, the war had been declared; forty-two days after his death, the war ended.

News of the tragedy at Kettle Hill reached Pauline O'Neill as she stepped off a train, returning to Prescott from a visit in a neighboring town. The stationmaster handed her the telegram and, as she later recalled, "kind hands and loving hearts led me home. The agony was so great that I could not weep for days."

Jim McClintock wrote to Pauline: "The grave is in a beautiful mountain valley. At the head is a tree, on which has been deeply carved the name and date. Around him are a numerous company of our brave fellows in their last sleep."

The news of Mayor O'Neill's death caused a wave of distress in Prescott and throughout the Territory. Newspapermen hurried to their desks to compose the most glowing of obituaries —many of them containing such praise as Buckey never had heard while courting politics in Arizona. The *Arizona Republican* summed it all up by writing, "One of Arizona's modern heroes, his name will live and be spoken with reverence as long as the Territory shall live."

Pauline was deluged with letters and telegrams of condolence and visited by all in Prescott with the tenderest of messages. One of the most touching letters came from the Negro citizens of Phoenix, perhaps motivated by Buckey's renowned attempt to save the two black troopers who had fallen into the slashing surf at Daiquiri. The wire expressed the most profound sorrow at Captain O'Neill's death, saying all had lost "a true and tried friend, the territory one of its foremost citizens, the Army of the United States a gallant officer, and his family a devoted husband and indulgent father."

Others who knew Buckey expressed their feelings in similiar terms. Fightin' Joe Wheeler, stricken with fever on the day of the San Juan battle, said, "As for Captain O'Neill, his loss is one of the severest that could have befallen the regiment. He was a man of cool head, great executive capacity, and literally dauntless courage."

In his *Autobiography*, Theodore Roosevelt recalled with great and poignant regret, "I freely sent the men for whom I cared most to where death might smite them; and death often smote them—as it did the two best officers in my regiment, Allyn Capron and Bucky O'Neill." And, in 1899, Roosevelt wrote, "A stanchly loyal and generous friend, he was also exceedingly ambitious on his own account. If, by risking his life, no matter how great the risk, he could gain high military distinction, he was bent on gaining it. He had taken so many chances when death lay on the hazard, that he felt the odds were now against him; but he said, 'Who would not risk his life for a star?' Had he lived, and had the war lasted, he would surely have won the eagle, if not the star."

Roosevelt's statement about the "star" was well-intentioned but incorrectly interpreted. In later years, certain writers—Jim McClintock and Roosevelt chief among them—would confuse this "star" with the star of a brigadier general. But in a letter published in the *New York Journal* two weeks after his death, written while he underwent training in San Antonio to his friend Thurlow Weed Barnes, Buckey had closed with the line, "Who would not gamble for a new star *in the flag?*" This line would become his epitaph.

Edward Marshall, who knew Captain O'Neill in the days leading up to the action at Las Guasimas, also gave his personal views on Buckey's character. His perhaps is a truer view than that offered by the ordinary adoring, well-meaning post-mortems. Marshall wrote:

O'Neill was the biggest, laziest, handsomest, officer in the regiment. His good-nature knew no bounds. He tried to keep up a strict military discipline among his men, but they did more to keep it up than he did, simply because they knew he wanted them to, and because they knew that he would never be harsh enough to them to demand it. . . . He did everything for his men and very little for himself. He rather hated to have them salute him than otherwise. He always dreaded the possibility of taking advantage of his rank.

In the spring of 1899, a party headed by Buckey's brothers Eugene and John Bernard went with Captain L. B. Alexander of Phoenix and the Reverend Henry A. Brown of Prescott to the San Juan battlefield to find Buckey's body. Brown, the

Rough Riders' regimental chaplain, had supervised burial the previous July 1. Traveling to the scene by carriage, Chaplain Brown located the shallow grave in the meadow below Kettle Hill in less than two hours of searching, and the body was disinterred. It was described as being "in a good state of preservation." Positive identification was not difficult: in the tunic pocket, Chaplain Brown found the black celluloid matchcase Jim McClintock had given Buckey, half jokingly, in San Antonio.

Buckey's pocket watch, an American Waltham, had stopped at four-seventeen, more than six hours after his death.

Buckey's remains were returned to Washington, scene of so many of his childhood experiences, and at two o'clock in the afternoon of May 1, 1899, with nearly two hundred persons present, he reached his final resting place in Arlington National Cemetery. There he joined his father, Captain John Owen O'Neill, who had been buried with his Civil War comrades just a year and a half previously.

Three volleys were fired by a military squad; the Reverend Father Donahue of St. Peter's Church conducted the Catholic services at the gravesite. Throughout the afternoon ceremony, as shadows lengthened on the gravestones and monuments to war dead, the sound of drumtaps mingled with the rifle fire and droning of somber voices.

The grave lies among those of his fellow Rough Riders in the topmost section of Arlington, about fifty yards beyond the Old Custis-Lee Mansion. Facing the roadway, the inscription on his handsome granite marker, below crossed cavalry sabers, reads:

WILLIAM OWEN O'NEILL
Mayor of Prescott, Arizona
Capt. Troop A, First U.S. Vol. Cav. Rough Riders
Brevet Major
Born Feb. 2, 1860
Killed July 1, 1898, at San Juan Hill, Cuba
"Who Would Not Die for a New Star in the Flag."

Solon Hannibal Borglum's statue of Buckey O'Neill at the Yavapai County Courthouse, Prescott, Arizona.

Epilogue

PAULINE O'NEILL married Buckey's younger brother, Eugene Brady O'Neill, on May 16, 1901 in Phoenix. The marriage apparently was a successful one, although Eugene's career in Arizona Territory bore controversial scars not unlike those of his hero brother. In fact, as late as 1912, a Douglas, Arizona, newspaper ran a story about Eugene headed "Political Polecat in Douglas," which included such remarks as these:

> . . . a political polecat . . . conceded to be the most foul mouthed individual that ever appeared on the public rostrum in Arizona. . . . This political skunk has been trying to land himself in some political office ever since he came into possession of the fortune of his brother, the immortal "Bucky" O'Neil [sic], the hero of San Juan Hill . . . habitue of the gambling houses and dance halls of Prescott. For ten years he was an aspirant for congress, but never was able to make any headway . . . poses as a reformer . . . understood to show that statehood had been secured by his individual effort. . . . This was so disgusting that he was promptly repudiated by the people and came in fifth in the primary race for United States senator . . . limber-jawed blatherskite.

If the item were clipped out, slightly edited, and placed in Buckey's scrapbook for the period of his delegate races of 1894 and 1896, no one would guess that the libels were not written for him but for his brother.

Eugene died tragically, an apparent suicide, in Los Angeles in July, 1917.

Mary O'Neill, Buckey's mother, died on September 14, 1914. Although little is known of her, one can guess she took great pride in her son's singular accomplishments in faraway Arizona, recognized in his own lifetime and hers and greatly commemorated after his hero's death in Cuba.

Pauline, it would appear, lived comfortably for the better part of her extraordinarily long life. Buckey is believed to have left her something like $200,000 in life insurance, Phoenix property, and savings from his onyx-mining venture. Remarkably, she applied for a widow's pension in 1954—56 years after Buckey's death—which may indicate that she had fallen on difficult times. She died on January 14, 1961, the day following her 96th birthday.

Buckey's only son, Maurice, died in the same month and year as his mother, at the Veteran's Hospital in Sawtelle, California. His business life concerned oil leasing and real estate in California. He was a veteran of World War One and had retired from his business career in 1956.

The two men who, with Buckey, had been the driving force behind the Arizona contingent of the Rough Riders had distinguished careers after the Spanish-American War. Alexander Oswald Brodie, on July 1, 1902, received from President Theodore Roosevelt the appointment as governor of Arizona Territory. Brodie filled this position until February 4, 1905, when he resigned to go to Washington for a post with the Records and Pension Office. In 1905, promoted to lieutenant colonel, he was assigned as military secretary and adjutant general of the Department of Visayas, Philippines. Returning to the United States in 1907, he served as adjutant general in the Department of Dakotas until 1911. He retired in 1913 and spent his last years in Haddonfield, New Jersey, with his wife and two sons. Brodie died there on May 11, 1918, and was buried with a sprig of Scottish heather in his clasped hands.

Jim McClintock, Buckey's friend, confidant, and match-provider extraordinary, returned to Arizona after the war and served as colonel of the First Arizona Infantry, president and historian of the Rough Riders Association, postmaster of Phoenix (1902-1914, 1928-1933); state historian (1919-1923), and Republican candidate for the U.S. Senate in 1922—which, following in Buckey's footsteps, he lost. McClintock died on May 10, 1934.

Nine years after Buckey's death, the imposing Remington-esque statue, commemorating the Arizona Rough Riders and their chief hero, Buckey O'Neill, was unveiled on the north side of the Yavapai County Courthouse grounds, near where the volunteers had gathered before entraining for San Antonio in May, 1898.

The idea for the monument seems to have originated with M. J. Hickey of Prescott, a close friend of Buckey's. Hickey was joined in setting up a special monument commission by other citizens who secured from the Territorial Legislature in 1905 an appropriation of ten thousand dollars to help pay for it. To this amount was added money from private donations—among them one described as "generous" from President Theodore Roosevelt.

Solon Hannibal Borglum, brother of Gutzon Borglum, the great Mount Rushmore artist, received the commission to cast the monument in bronze. The resulting work was a Borglum masterpiece.

On July 3, 1907, a parade over a mile long wound through the streets of Prescott, led by the Fifth Cavalry Band and fol-lowed by a cavalry troop from Fort Whipple. Then came a troop of Rough Riders; Civil War veterans; the fire departments of Phoenix, Tucson, and Prescott; a procession of Knights of Columbus; members of the Monument Commission, and Terri-torial Governor Joseph H. Kibbey and his staff; prominent citizens of the Territory; and military officers. The entire city bedecked itself in red, white, and blue bunting; flags flew from every storefront and window.

As the parade ended, some seven thousand persons gathered at the monument, which was covered with a canvas shroud, to hear Governor Kibbey's remarks. Colonel James H. McClintock said a few words; then the sculptor, Solon Borglum, was intro-duced, followed by other dignitaries. Maurice O'Neill, Buckey's son, stepped forward, just before noon, and pulled the ropes that dropped the shroud from the monument.

Although the statue was erected "To the Memory of Captain

William O. O'Neill" and "In Honor Of" the Rough Riders, many
felt then, as they do now, that the figure seated on the straining,
uprearing horse, so finely wrought in golden brown bronze, was
Buckey O'Neill himself.

No one who sees the magnificent statue in the Prescott courthouse yard today can be unaffected by it. The mind races to
find out who "Captain William O. O'Neill" was, and what
particular exploit guaranteed him such sculptured immortality.
And no one troubling to find out *who* William O. O'Neill was
has any trouble in understanding *why* he looks out over his
town, even now, nearly three-quarters of a century after he fell
in faraway Cuba.

SOURCES

THERE ARE FEW W. O. O'Neill papers per se, although a scattering of his letters (mainly to his friend James McClintock) are on file with the Arizona Historical Society in Tucson. A valuable source of material on O'Neill is the McClintock Papers in the Phoenix Public Library; and the Sharlot Hall Museum in Prescott has made a valiant effort over the years to collect O'Neill photographs, newspaper clippings, and other items. In addition, a considerable mass of paper on O'Neill, as well as on John O'Neill, can be found in the National Archives. These, while consisting mostly of war service records, contain documents pertaining to pension petitions and the adoption of Maurice O'Neill by Buckey and Pauline.

CHAPTER ONE

Getting to Know the Territory

On Arizona territorial history: Jay J. Wagoner, *Arizona Territory, 1863-1912: A Political History* (Tucson, Arizona, 1970); Douglas Martin, *An Arizona Chronology: The Territorial Years* (Tucson, 1963); Odie B. Faulk, *Arizona: A Short History* (Norman, Oklahoma, 1970); Howard R. Lamar, *The Far Southwest, 1846-1912: A Territorial History* (New Haven, Connecticut, 1966); James H. McClintock, *Arizona: Prehistoric, Aboriginal, Pioneer, Modern* (Chicago, Illinois, 1916).

On Frémont's governorship: Allan Nevins, *Fremont: Pathmaker of the West* (New York, 1955); Wagoner, *Arizona Territory*.

On the origin of "Buckey" as a nickname, all sources seem to agree with McClintock, who wrote often of his best friend in the years between the end of the Spanish-American War and his death in 1934. Letters from O'Neill to McClintock were always signed "Buckey"—with the *e*. McClintock Papers, Phoenix Public Library.

On Henry Garfias: Obituary in the *Phoenix Herald*, cited by Maurice Kildare ["Fastest Gun in Phoenix" (*Frontier Times*, December-January, 1967-1968)]. Garfias retired in May, 1896. A short time later his horse spooked and fell on him and he died as a result of the injuries.

CHAPTER TWO

The O'Neills of Ireland and America

On John O'Neill: When he died on January 13, 1897, his age was given as sixty-three years five months. Papers in the National Archives, all related to his Civil War record, wound, pension, and death, contain no hint as to his precise birthplace in Ireland, immigration, or occupation before 1862. Other information gleaned from documents from the Record and Pension Office (War Department), company muster rolls, casualty sheets, and official letters in the National Archives; *Portrait and Biographical Record of Arizona* (Chicago, 1901); St. Clair Mulholland, *The Story of the 116th Regiment, Pennsylvania Infantry* (Philadelphia, 1899); letter dated March 12, 1947, State Library, Harrisburg, Pennsylvania, to Alice Metzger of the Sharlot Hall Museum in Prescott (Sharlot Hall Museum Archives).

On Irish emigration in the mid-nineteenth century: Carl Wittke, *The Irish in America* (Baton Rouge, Louisiana, 1956); Stephen Byrne, *Irish Emigration to the United States* (New York, 1969).

On Mary McMenimin: *Portrait and Biographical Record of Arizona* says her paternal grandfather was "engaged in farming near Philadelphia and died in his 99th year."

On Meagher and the Irish Brigade: Robert G. Athearn, *Thomas Francis Meagher: An Irish Revolutionary in America* (Boulder, Colorado, 1949); Vorin E. Whan, *Fiasco at Fredericksburg* (State College, Pennsylvania, 1961); Mulholland, *The Story of the 116th Regiment.*

On William O. O'Neill's birthplace: Throughout his life Buckey O'Neill listed St. Louis, Missouri, as his birthplace but at least two records indicate Ireland instead. Charles Herner, in his *The Arizona Rough Riders* (Tucson, Arizona, 1970), points out that when O'Neill signed the muster-in rolls in San Antonio, Texas, in May, 1898, "Ireland" was placed in the space marked "Where Born." The author of the present work, in attempting to shed some light on this odd circumstance, discovered another document in the records of the Adjutant General's Office, War Department, National Archives— dated January 6, 1899—which lists Ireland as place of birth. It appears, however, that this paper's information was drawn solely from the muster-in roll. A third piece of evidence, "The Great Register of Yavapai County, Arizona Territory," for October 14, 1884 (copy in Sharlot Hall Museum), lists William O. O'Neill, as "Age 25 [*sic*], *Native of Ireland,* Local Residence Prescott. *Naturalized by father's naturalization*" (emphasis added). On the other hand, the U.S. Census for Phoenix, Maricopa County, Arizona Territory, taken on June 10, 1880, lists William O. O'Neill's birthplace as "Missouri." Buckey's wife, Pauline, when she belatedly filed for a widow's pension in 1954, listed her husband's birthplace as "St. Louis, Mo." ("Application for Compensation or Pension by Widow or Child," dated

April 1. 1954, W. O. O'Neill files, National Archives). James H. McClintock, one of O'Neill's closest friends from the time both men settled in Arizona in 1879 throughout the Cuban campaign of 1898, invariably listed his friend's birthplace as St. Louis in the many letters about Buckey that he wrote following the war, and in both newspaper articles and speeches (McClintock Papers; also his *Arizona: Prehistoric, Aboriginal, Pioneer, Modern*). Much of the evidence pointing toward a St. Louis, or at least a U.S., place of birth for their son hinges on the date and place of John O'Neill's and Mary McMenimin's marriage. Sound confirmation of John O'Neill's date of arrival in the United States, his business ventures, prosperity, or indeed any factual data of his career prior to the Civil War, is lacking. It is impossible, therefore, to dismiss the possibility that his oldest son was born in Ireland, perhaps during a "trip home" (as suggested by Charles Herner in a letter to the author, February 21, 1971) that John and Mary might have made between their marriage in October, 1858, and Buckey's birth in February, 1860.

On Buckey's education: Virtually all who have written about O'Neill credit him with having obtained a law degree from either Georgetown University, George Washington University, or National University. In fact, there are no records of O'Neill's having attended any of those institutions. (Letters to the author from the registrars, archivists, and historians of Georgetown and George Washington universities, January-March, 1971. National University existed in Washington, D.C., from 1869-1954 when it became a part of GWU.) James McClintock apparently believed at one time that Buckey had a college education but never seems to have been convinced that his friend was a bona fide lawyer. Among several statements to this effect to be found in the McClintock Papers is a letter, dated just before his death in 1934, to Edward L. O'Malley of Phoenix, in which McClintock says, "I doubt that he was admitted to the bar though I do know that he was a qualified legal shorthand reporter."

CHAPTER THREE
Stopover in Tombstone

On Tombstone, Shieffelin, Clum. and others: Douglas Martin, *The Tombstone Epitaph* (Albuquerque, New Mexico, 1951): Richard O'Connor, *Bat Masterson* (New York, 1957); John M. Myers. *The Tombstone Story* (New York, 1950); Odie B. Faulk, *Tombstone: Myth and Reality* (New York, 1972).

CHAPTER FOUR
A Wandering Interlude

On where Buckey went and what he did, 1881-1882: Ralph Keithley, *Buckey O'Neill* (Caldwell, Idaho, 1949); clipping, undated, "How Buckey O'Neill Got His Famous Sobriquet," in McClintock Papers; Joseph Miller, ed., *Arizona Cavalcade* (New York, 1962).

CHAPTER FIVE
New Customer on Whiskey Row

On Prescott history: Richard J. Hinton, *The Handbook of Arizona* (Tucson, 1954); Henry G. Alsberg and Harry Hansen, *Arizona, the Grand Canyon State* (New York, 1966); Miller, *Arizona Cavalcade;* Wagoner, *Arizona Territory, 1863-1912.*

On Frémont and Gosper: Wagoner, *Arizona Territory.* Frémont lived the rest of his life at Tarrytown-on-the-Hudson and died in New York City on July 13, 1890, at the age of seventy-seven.

On Whiskey Row: The *Prescott Courier* for May 15, 1964 (centennial edition) gives a long and excellent history of the Row and its establishments.

CHAPTER SIX
The Bloodiest Day in Court

On the courtroom ruckus: Several good accounts exist, including those in Wagoner, *Arizona Territory;* Joseph Miller, *Arizona, the Last Frontier* (New York, 1956); *Prescott Courier,* May 15, 1964 (centennial edition); clipping files in O'Neill Papers, Arizona Historical Society, Tucson; contemporary newspaper accounts.

CHAPTER SEVEN
Hoof and Horn and a Dun for the Thirteenth

On the *Hoof and Horn*: files of the paper in Sharlot Hall Museum archives.

On the Thirteenth Legislative Assembly: Wagoner's *Arizona Territory;* Martin, *Arizona Chronology.*

CHAPTER EIGHT
Pauline and the Rubicon of Bachelorhood

On the marriage to Pauline: Keithley, *Buckey O'Neill* (the author interviewed Pauline O'Neill in the 1940's); transcripts of *Hoof and*

Horn columns in Arizona Historical Society files and newspaper files in Sharlot Hall Museum; clippings and letters in McClintock Papers.

CHAPTER NINE
The Hanging of Dennis Dilda

On the Dilda case: Will C. Barnes, "When a Brave Man Fainted," in *Echoes of the Past: Tales of Old Yavapai* (Prescott, Arizona, 1964); contemporary newspaper accounts and the *Prescott Courier* for May 15, 1964; McClintock Papers.

On Buckey's story, "A Horse of the Hash-Knife Brand": Newspaper clipping of the story in the O'Neill Papers.

CHAPTER TEN
A Soft Berth for Judge O'Neill

On Whipple Barracks acquaintances: William A. Glassford to James McClintock, letter, February 1, 1915, McClintock Papers.

On the race for the probate judgeship: Contemporary newspaper accounts, transcriptions from newspapers outside Prescott in the O'Neill files of the Arizona Historical Society.

CHAPTER ELEVEN
Buckey-of-all-Trades

On the birth of Buckey, Jr.: *Prescott Journal-Miner*, January 5, 1887, through May 11, 1887.

On the Whiskey Row fires: *Prescott Journal-Miner*, April 6, 1886; *Prescott Courier*, centennial edition, May 15, 1964. On July 4, 1900, after a long drought, a fire broke out in a hotel on Montezuma and Goodwin, spread along Whiskey Row, burning three and a half city blocks and causing 1 million to 1.5 million dollars in damages to business and residential properties. Volunteers dynamited buildings in the fire's path to stop its progress.

On Buckey's interest in irrigation, tourism, etc.: McClintock Papers, O'Neill Papers in Sharlot Hall Museum.

CHAPTER TWELVE
The Conquistador of Yavapai County

On the sheriff's race: contemporary newspaper accounts, particularly the *Prescott Courier*, September 10-November 8, 1888, *Prescott Journal-Miner*, and *Phoenix Herald*.

CHAPTER THIRTEEN

Long Ride from Diablo Canyon

On the robbery and chase: in addition to the newspaper accounts, Keithley, *Buckey O'Neill*; Will C. Barnes, "The Canyon Diablo Train Robbery," *Arizona Historical Review*, April, 1930; Dan Harvick (as told to William Sparks), "Canyon Diablo Train Robbery" *Frontier Times*, December-January, 1970-1971).

CHAPTER FOURTEEN

Calamity on Walnut Creek

On the flood: Pat Savage, *One Last Frontier* (New York, 1964); Nell Murbarger, *Ghosts of Adobe Walls* (Los Angeles, 1964); contemporary newspaper accounts including those in Prescott and the *Arizona Weekly Enterprise* (Florence) from May 18, 1889; letters and clippings in McClintock Papers and O'Neill Papers.

CHAPTER FIFTEEN

A Tax for the Iniquitous Railroad

On the "A and P Letter": the complete letter in the O'Neill Papers in Sharlot Hall Museum, Prescott; Wagoner, *Arizona Territory*; the *Arizona Weekly Enterprise*, August 9, 1890.

CHAPTER SIXTEEN

Onyx, Silver, and Copper

On the onyx venture: McClintock Papers, Phoenix Public Library.

On the Grand Canyon interest: *Portrait and Biographical Record of Arizona*; Edwin Corle, *Listen, Bright Angel* (New York, 1946); O'Neill Papers.

On bolting the party, free silver, etc.: Wagoner, *Arizona Territory*; McClintock, *Arizona*; *Arizona Republican*, August 21, 1893; *Arizona Weekly Enterprise*, July 29, 1892; O'Neill Papers, Sharlot Hall Museum.

CHAPTER SEVENTEEN

The Populist Candidate of 1894

On the Populist movement: George B. Tindall, *A Populist Reader* (New York, 1966); Robert F. Durden, *The Climax of Populism: The Election of 1896* (Lexington, Kentucky, 1965); Mark Sullivan, *Our Times* (New York, 1937).

The Open Letter: full copy of letter in O'Neill Papers, Sharlot Hall Museum.

CHAPTER EIGHTEEN

The Populist Candidate of 1896

Besides the usual contemporary newspaper accounts of this campaign, an important account is found in the *Arizona Republican* dated May 31, 1907, and headed "A Hero's Memorial, A Story of Bucky O'Neill." Also the *Arizona Stock Journal*, October 23, 1896; McClintock, *Arizona*; O'Neill Papers.

CHAPTER NINETEEN

The Populist Mayor of Prescott

On John O'Neill's death: Adjutant General's Office, War Department, National Archives.

On Buckey and the single tax: McClintock Papers, correspondence between O'Neill and McClintock.

On the prison labor contract: Wagoner's *Arizona Territory*; McClintock, *Arizona*.

On the adoption: the entire set of adoption papers is with the W. O. O'Neill records in the National Archives.

CHAPTER TWENTY

Remember the *Maine*!

On Weyler, the Cuban junta, the prewar days: Charles H. Brown, *The Correspondents' War* (New York, 1967); Frank Freidel, *Splendid Little War* (Boston, 1958); Jack C. Dierks, *A Leap to Arms* (New York, 1970); Margaret Leech, *In the Days of McKinley* (New York, 1959); Walter Millis, *The Martial Spirit* (Cambridge, Massachusetts, 1931).

On the *Maine* tragedy: Gregory Mason, *Remember the Maine!* (New York, 1939) plus sources previously cited.

On Buckey, McClintock, Brodie, and plans to volunteer: Herner, *The Arizona Rough Riders*; O'Neill to McClintock, letters, in McClintock Papers.

CHAPTER TWENTY-ONE

The Cowboy Regiment

On preparations in Prescott and the Territory: Herner, *The Arizona Rough Riders*; V. C. Jones, *Roosevelt's Rough Riders* (New

York, 1971); Edward Marshall, *The Story of the Rough Riders* (New York, 1899); Clifford P. Westermeier. *Who Rush to Glory, The Cowboy Volunteers of 1898* (Caldwell, Idaho, 1958); A. D. Webb, "Arizonans in the Spanish-American War," *Arizona Historical Review*, January, 1929.

CHAPTER TWENTY-TWO
Off to War

On Governor McCord's address: Wagoner, *Arizona Territory*. McCord resigned the governorship in August to command the First Territorial Volunteer Infantry Regiment but the unit never left the country. He became a U.S. marshal (1901-1905) and at the time of his death in 1908, was customs collector at Nogales. He claimed never to have regretted his decision to resign the governorship.

On the mascot: A small controversy exists here over the name of the female mountain lion donated by Robert Brow. Roosevelt later recalled the name as Josephine; however, Edward Marshall. in *The Story of the Rough Riders*, claims Florence was the name given the cat at Prescott. Will Henry, in a footnote in his well-researched novel, *San Juan Hill* (New York, 1962), says Florence was the name and his authority was Brow himself.

On the Tom Rynning rivalry: Tom Rynning. *Gun-Notches* (New York, 1931).

On arrival in San Antonio: John C. Rayburn, "The Rough Riders in San Antonio," *Arizona and the West*, Summer. 1961; Herner. *The Arizona Rough Riders*.

CHAPTER TWENTY-THREE
The Rough Riders

On the training period. makeup. and personality of the regiment: In addition to previously cited sources: Theodore Roosevelt, *The Rough Riders* (New York. 1900), and *Autobiography* (New York. 1925); Hermann Hagedorn, *Leonard Wood: A Biography* (New York. 1931); Henry F. Pringle. *Theodore Roosevelt* (New York. 1956); the *San Antonio Daily Light*, May 15-26. 1898.

CHAPTER TWENTY-FOUR
Chaos in Tampa

On the Tampa interlude. in addition to sources previously cited: Irving Werstein. *1898: The Spanish-American War* (New York,

1966); John P. Dyer, *"Fightin' Joe" Wheeler* (University, Louisiana, 1941); Herbert H. Sargent, *The Campaign of Santiago de Cuba* (Chicago, 1907); D. L. W., interview with Frank C. Brito of Las Cruces, New Mexico, a member of Troop I, which remained in Tampa during the campaign; A. C. M. Azoy, *Charge! The Story of the Battle of San Juan Hill* (New York, 1961); Tom Hall, *The Fun and Fighting of the Rough Riders* (New York, 1899).

CHAPTER TWENTY-FIVE

Daiquiri and Las Guasimas

On the landings and first battle, in addition to previously cited sources: Richard Harding Davis, "The Battle of San Juan," *Scribner's Magazine*, October, 1898; Edward Marshall, "The Santiago Campaign," *Scribner's Magazine*, September, 1898.

CHAPTER TWENTY-SIX

Up to Kettle Hill

On Buckey's remark about the Spanish bullet: This occurs in virtually all accounts of O'Neill's death and the authenticity is strengthened by the testimony of Jesse Langdon, a member of Lieutenant Woodbury Kane's Troop K, who was an eyewitness to Buckey's death and who is the last surviving member of the Rough Rider regiment (Jesse D. Langdon, to D. L. W., letter, January 23, 1971).

CHAPTER TWENTY-SEVEN

Death Was the Black Horse

On the details of Buckey's death: Jesse D. Langdon to D. L. W., letters containing eyewitness account; *Arizona Republican*, July 26, 1898; Herner, *The Arizona Rough Riders*.

On William Pulsing's testimony: This must be regarded carefully, although the details seem authentic. Described as a "German-American businessman from New Orleans who was accepted into the regiment largely on the basis of his regular army experience," Pulsing was a patient at the Red Cross Hospital on Long Island when he told his story. Contrary to the *New York Times* account, however, Pulsing was not a member of O'Neill's troop, nor is he listed in the muster-out roll of Roosevelt's *The Rough Riders*. It is possible that he was a member of the First Regular Cavalry, deployed on the left of the Rough Riders below Kettle Hill. Pulsing seems to have known a great deal about Buckey's career before the Cuban campaign, but where he got his information is a mystery. See the *New York Times*, September 19, 1898.

On the San Juan Hill assault: Jesse D. Langdon to D. L. W., letter, January 23, 1971, and subsequent correspondence.

On Buckey's watch: The watch is on display today in the Sharlot Hall Museum in Prescott, where it is mistakenly identified as showing "the time of his death on San Juan Hill."

On the Arlington ceremonies: *Washington Post*, May 2, 1899; McClintock Papers.

Epilogue

On Eugene O'Neill: clippings and documents in McClintock Papers; on his death, Maurice O. O'Neill, Jr., to D. L. W., letter, March 11, 1971.

On Maurice O'Neill and Pauline O'Neill: D. L. W. correspondence with Maurice O'Neill, Jr., Phoenix, Arizona, March, 1971.

INDEX

Page numbers of illustrations are in italics